A GUIDE TO

TIDAL POOLS OF THE WESTERN CAPE

Explore 34 of the region's most beautiful pools

SERAI DOWLING

FOREWORD BY JUSTIN FOX

First published in 2024 by Rockhopper Books

Production management by Serai Dowling
Typeset and layout by Tania Bester
Edited by Lesley Hay-Whitton
Proofread by Lauren Smith
Indexed by Naya Lizardo

ISBN 978 0796131478

Rockhopper Books
Unit A Victory Park
Capricorn Business Park
Muizenberg
7945

'It is advisable to look from the tide pool to the stars
and then back to the tide pool again.'

— *The Log from the Sea of Cortez*, John Steinbeck, 1951

Southern periwinkle *(Afrolittorina knysnaensis)*, a type of sea snail

Contents

Dwarf cushion stars *(Parvulastra exigua)* found at Glencairn Tidal Pool

Foreword

In the realms where land meets sea, where waves sculpt rock into intricate forms and tides unveil hidden treasures, lies the enigmatic tidal pools of our coastal landscape. These sanctuaries, set beside a tempestuous ocean, invite us to pause, reflect and reconnect with a natural world too often overlooked in the maelstrom of modern life.

Much like the *inkommer* from Gauteng who, with fresh eyes, unveils these oft-unnoticed gems of the Western Cape, this guidebook bids us to gaze anew into the shimmering depths of tidal pools. Serai blends poetic reverence with scientific insight to reveal the profound significance of these watery havens.

For a hundred thousand years, our ancestors lived along this coast, foraging from and swimming in its rock pools. Indeed, these shores have provided the perfect place, with the perfect food, for *Homo sapiens* to develop. The shell middens dotting our beaches attest to the bounty of the intertidal zone, first harvested by early humans and later by Khoisan, while the stone *visvywer* traps (to catch bigger fish on the outgoing tide) speak of the advanced fishing methods of more recent inhabitants. The modern tidal pool is a descendant of these sites and our fascination with them stretches back to the origin of our species. Their glassy green eyes provide a window into our distant past.

Romantic poets such as Coleridge, Byron and Keats loved swimming in wild environments as it allowed them to connect with nature and nourish their creativity, find spiritual inspiration and engage with the sublime. Their obsession was called hydromania and, two centuries later, swimming in natural pools is more popular than ever. In the icy waters of the Western Cape, it has the same touch of sublime madness.

As we immerse ourselves in Serai's meticulously researched narratives, we are transported not only through the histories and ecosystems these pools nurture but also through their profound cultural and ecological importance. They are more than mere geological and man-made formations; they are portals to our shared past, guardians of coastal heritage and oases of solace in an often chaotic world.

Serai's passion for these pools is palpable, each page a celebration of her enchantment and a call to preserve their beauty for generations to come. Her exploration transcends documentation; it becomes a journey of spiritual renewal, a reminder of our interconnectedness with the natural world and the responsibility we bear as stewards of our planet.

In an era shadowed by environmental concerns and societal disconnection, the significance of these pools begins to emerge: they are not just places to visit but spaces that inspire a sense of wonder and foster a deep appreciation for our surroundings. Through Serai's lens, they become catalysts for introspection and for change, urging us to forge a more harmonious relationship with our environment.

As you embark on this journey through the pages of Serai's work, may you too find yourself captivated by the allure of tidal pools, and inspired to join the ranks of those who champion their preservation. For in these hidden marvels lies not only the promise of physical rejuvenation but also the potential for spiritual awakening – a reminder that, amid the ebb and flow of life, nature's gifts endure, waiting to be cherished and protected.

This book is truly a labour of love, capturing the allure of these spaces and brimming with information about their history, fauna, flora, geology and adjacent sights. Serai helps the reader to better understand these watery worlds, our relationship with them (both past and present) and what this could mean for our mental health, for nation-building and for the protection and conservation of our oceans.

Welcome to a voyage of discovery, where each turn of the page reveals a realm of wonder beneath our very noses – a world where the timeless beauty of tidal pools meets the boundless curiosity of the human spirit.

Justin Fox, June 2024

Preface

Tidal pools are a haven, a sanctuary. They act as connectors: of humans to the natural world from which we grow increasingly disconnected; to each other, across cultural divides; to peace and respite from a country or society in flux. As we grapple with place-making and meaning in South Africa, the tidal pools – with their rich and diverse history, remarkable sea life and protected spaces – offer the opportunity to remake and reclaim spaces that include 'the other'. Today these pools are a place of connection and joy, as swimmers immerse themselves in the icy waters of the Southern Atlantic Ocean.

The word 'holy' has its roots in Old English, with its origin traced back to the Proto-Germanic word 'hailaga' or 'heilag', which means 'whole' or 'uninjured'. This root is also related to the Old High German word 'heilag', meaning 'holy' or 'sacred'. When we lose that sense of connection, that sense of belonging to the sanctity of life, we are left less whole. Perhaps if we thought of tidal pools as repositories for holy things, we might treat them with the respect they deserve, not least of all for the joyous creatures they shelter (and that includes us).

I know the pools intimately, having spent many hours in each. I know where the urchins like to cluster in Dalebrook, and where the starfish are partial to gathering in Kalk Bay 2. I've watched whales breach off the shore from the rock at the heart of Miller's Point (which itself is shaped like a heart, if viewed from above), and shared a lone swim with a gannet at Buffels Bay in Cape Point Nature Reserve. My love for these pools is tangible and real. Through this book I hope to foster in you a desire to explore, love, conserve and protect all of them and to discover for yourself the deep sense of peace they foster.

Humans have long enjoyed a relationship with the sea, and tidal pools in particular offer safe, fluid, fertile places for humans to experience the ocean, learn to swim and engage with intertidal zone creatures at leisure. They're places where we all – birds, fish, humans, limpets and others – can peacefully coexist. It was with delight that my existing love of the natural world was extended to that of the sea through my deep and now abiding love of tidal pools. I discovered a world of wonder: from tentacled whatsits, hard-shelled thingamabobs and spiky doodads to flashing silvery fish and seaweeds … they all held me in their thrall and invited me to know them better. And so I said yes to the invitation and dived in to better explore and understand these watery worlds, our human relationship to them (both past and present) and what this could all mean for our mental health, nation-building and the protection and conservation of our oceans. And along the way, I learnt the names and natures of the creatures I once (rudely) referred to as whatsits, thingamabobs and doodads.

It is my contention that the more time you spend in the ocean, the more she reclaims you – the more time she wants with you, and the more likely you are to want to swim in her depths. This sentiment seems to be echoed by Heraclitus, who observed more than two thousand years ago: 'For souls it is joy or death to become wet'. Maybe he meant solely the rejuvenating quality of water, or something more indirect – the constant flux of existence or the interdependence of everything – but my own love for the ocean deepened through my time spent at tidal pools.

I started swimming in tidal pools many moons ago. Time spent bobbing about in their waters led to more time in different tidal pools, eventually turning into swimming laps and gaining fitness. As I gazed into the water while my body sliced through its cool embrace, I developed a deepening curiosity about the sea life I observed. Their beauty entranced me: the odd nudibranch bursting vibrantly into view, shoals of silvery fish glinting in the afternoon sunlight, an octopus shyly gliding from one rocky nook to another on a cloudy afternoon. There was a whole world to learn about, and to share. I'd invite hosts of people to join me on my almost-daily sunrise expeditions. There were few takers but my reputation as An Extremely Odd Person grew among my friends. And at the pools themselves, I met like-minded regulars who were equally taken with some aspect of the tidal pools.

I've spent many an afternoon getting knocked off the back wall of Dalebrook by the incoming waves, laughing with strangers as we all enjoy the astounding beauty that surrounds us. I've met wonderful people who have shared their stories, at both the most and the least popular pools, and my experiences have convinced me that tidal pools in South Africa play an integral role in creating social connectedness and acting as a bridge between cultures, ages, socio-economic divides and races. Our country is so damaged by injustice and prejudice, and yet in the pools I've watched people come together in a way that you'd be hard-pressed to intentionally craft.

As a naturally curious person I researched the history of my favourite pools and learnt more about the marine life that enthralled me. I began venturing outside of Cape Town in search of more pools. When a list of the pools was shared on a WhatsApp swimming group, I decided to swim all of them. And then one cold spring afternoon at Dalebrook, after a joyous dip during a storm, a friend suggested I write a book about the tidal pools. I took up the challenge.

By sharing what I've learnt, I hope to increase knowledge of the beauty, history, cultural relevance and accessibility of the pools, and create more opportunities for people to connect.

Each of the tidal pools is distinctive in character, but also mercurial in nature, which makes capturing their essence impossible. On a sunny day, Dalebrook, for example, can be effervescent and welcoming. During a storm, it is tempestuous and beguiling. Venus Pool can seem like a treasure trove of beautiful sea creatures on a windless day at sunrise, but when the waves crash over the rocks and the wind picks up it can feel terrifying.

I hope, by exploring this guide, you'll be enticed to visit the pools not once but many times over, getting to know them as I do, in all their capricious and alluring beauty. And that, by doing so, you'll meet a host of people you wouldn't ordinarily encounter, and share with them the joy of tidal pool swimming.

The natural splendour to be found in and around the pools isn't limited to life below the surface. From the gulls above to the Cape clawless otters going about their business, the majesty calls us out of ourselves and offers relief from daily stressors. I have seen dippers arrive thoroughly prepared with flasks of coffee, woolly hats, dedicated towels for changing ...

all apparently distractions from the world around them. But when they leave the pools there is a lightness in their faces, eyes brighter for having immersed themselves in the cold water. We're invited out of ourselves – out of our busy heads – to appreciate the wonders of the world. No matter what our circumstances, tidal pools offer a natural embrace and respite.

In sharing information about some of the more common sea creatures and surrounding flora and fauna, I hope I'm able to help you identify and demystify things you have often seen; I also suggest books and resources that go into greater depth. We protect what we love, and maybe we'll do a better job of conserving and protecting these natural wonderlands if we know a little more about them: perhaps we'll switch to sea-friendly sunscreens, pick up our rubbish, leave the creatures be when we find them, and support environmentally friendly initiatives to clean the pools without chemicals.

My fervent desire is that, when you visit a tidal pool, you stop and take the time to see, feel and appreciate the beauty around you. Connect with it as you swim. Observe its positive impact on children as they play in the water. Notice the joy it brings to the elderly, who are able to access the sea without fear of being swept away, their fragility forgotten for a few minutes of weightless swimming. See how the cold water lifts your mood and makes you feel more alive. Is it not, then, a small thing for us to care for these spaces and hold each other to better behaviour when we see litter being dropped? These spaces are shared, not only with other humans, but also with other species, from which we are not separate. Our fate is the same as theirs. So, let us remember what it is to honour nature in all her glory, care for and protect her as she offers places and spaces for us to rest, recover and be revived in.

We're here for such a short time; let's celebrate that time by bearing witness to and loving the natural world. I hope this book invigorates to your desire to do so.

A dassie peers out from beneath a deck at Ficks Pool

Note

This book must, of necessity, employ the terminology associated with apartheid, particularly regarding the racial classifications that were enforced. At the initial level of differentiation, we find the categorisations 'white' and 'non-white'. The latter term serves as a comprehensive descriptor encompassing all people of colour.

There are notable inaccuracies between the spelling of the names of the pools in historical records and the signs that appear alongside them. For the purposes of the book I have chosen to align the spelling with the signage at each pool, rather than what it should be, based on research and archival evidence. However, where the evidence of the correct spelling is irrefutable, such as Woolley's Tidal Pool, I have chosen to use the correct spelling.

Small children should be supervised at all times near the ocean, along rocky shorelines and at the tidal pools.

Remember to prioritise safety, follow any local regulations and respect the marine environment at all times.

Miller's Point looks like a heart when viewed from above

An introduction to tidal pool swimming

Swimming in tidal pools is, for me, about joy, freedom and a sense of wonder. Swimming in a gym pool by comparison feels unnatural: tepid water and manky shared showers. This guide is an invitation to explore some of the most beautiful outdoor swimming spots in the world. Whether in sultry summers, when glistening azure waters welcome you, or in chilly winters when tumultuous seas tumble over the back wall, tidal pools in the Western Cape offer a splendid opportunity for adventure for young and old and those anywhere in between.

You'll discover pools nestled between giant boulders and along stretches of soft sandy beaches, punctuated only by gulls or the odd otter. You'll learn where spectacular natural pools welcome you in with a cool embrace, and swim at the foot of a massive mountain. You will dodge urchins on steps or sit quietly and watch as an octopus glides by – the pools are teeming with jewel-like sea creatures.

Tidal pools provide safe access for all, sheltering swimmers from rough seas and dangerous currents. In addition, tidal pools are cleaned out by the high tide twice a day. The resurgence in open-water swimming has meant that these pools have recently become more popular. When I started swimming in the Camps Bay Tidal Pool in 2013, it was just a dear friend and me, with a handful of other people and the gulls for company. Now we have to dodge the dippers, even at dawn! This is testimony to the pleasures to be had in these safe swimming zones. It perhaps also suggests the desire of the bathers to share the health benefits with friends and to immerse themselves in the natural splendours of the outdoors, particularly as our awareness of climate change becomes more acute.

The tidal pools of the Western Cape have a significant history and cultural relevance to their people, which is often overlooked or forgotten, and sometimes not even known. The pools haven't always been inclusive: local laws prohibited people of colour from using them.

It was only with the creation of the railways and intentional emulation of the popular coastal resorts of Britain's Brighton and Scarborough that Cape Town's tidal pool creation began. Fishermen created fish traps between rocky crags, and over time some of these were enclosed with walls and turned into bathing pools. In other instances, savvy sea bathers, seeking safe swimming, created their own pools.

Tidal pools link us safely to the sea, and also to other people. South Africa has a complicated past that bleeds into its current reality: both colonialism and apartheid shaped our history and silenced local voices. As a result, tidal pools in South Africa have a weightier cultural relevance than in other parts of the world. Their history is at once fascinating and complex, tainted by the colonists who brought the pools in their current format to this country, but who were also brutal gatekeepers of the geography of the landscape. Our pools today are largely poorly maintained, and yet they provide a backdrop for fun human connection and a sense of respite from the stressors of daily life. We are spoilt for choice, with an array of pools that are rich with sea life, historical depth and cultural relevance.

The advent and rise of outdoor swimming

The advent and rise of outdoor swimming in Britain from the 19th century to the present day has been marked by various trends, developments and cultural shifts. This timeline highlights key milestones and events during this period:

1815–1860s: The beginnings

- **1815:** Cleveland Pools in Bath is built. It is the oldest outdoor public pool in the UK.
- **1850s:** The concept of outdoor swimming gains greater popularity in Britain, primarily for health and exercise benefits.
- **1860:** The Serpentine Lake in London's Hyde Park becomes one of the first publicly accessible outdoor swimming locations.

Late 19th century: Pools and facilities

- **1880s:** The construction of the purpose-built outdoor swimming pools begins in various British cities, offering safer, more controlled environments for swimmers.

Early 20th century: The golden era

- **1930s:** This decade witnesses a golden era in the construction of lidos and outdoor swimming pools, with notable numbers of lidos opening across Britain.
- **1935:** The Edmonton Lido is the first open-air pool to be called a lido, from the Italian word for 'shore' or 'beach'. The Tinsdale Lido in Plymouth, designed by John Wibberley, is one of the notable lidos built in this period.

Mid-20th century: Post-war decline

- **1940s–1950s:** Some lidos and outdoor pools decline in popularity owing to post-war economic challenges and changing leisure preferences.
- **1960s:** Many lidos struggle to stay open, facing financial difficulties and maintenance issues. According to Michael Wood for the *Conversation,* 'The 1960 Wolfenden report, Sport and the Community and the 1968 Sports Council report Planning for Sport were catalysts for the demise of outdoor swimming pools in policy. The mandate was that "as a general rule, [pools] should be indoors"'.

1980s: Revival and restoration

- **1980s:** A renewed interest in outdoor swimming, coupled with historical preservation efforts, leads to the restoration of several lidos.

21st century: Resurgence and diversity

- **2000s:** A resurgence of interest in outdoor swimming, driven by health and fitness trends, contributes to the growth of wild swimming and open-water events, and the popularity of lidos.
- **2010s:** Open-water swimming events, such as the Swim Serpentine in Hyde Park and the Henley Classic, gain prominence.
- **2020s:** Outdoor swimming, including cold-water swimming and wild swimming, continues to grow in popularity, with enthusiasts enjoying natural bodies of water and organised events.

Inland spa culture – visiting lakes and baths away from the sea – had been popular for most of the 18th century, but it was Dr Richard Russell who was the first medical professional in the UK credited with extolling the virtues of seawater to treat physical ailments. Although his focus was primarily on the waters of Brighton, he is recognised for fuelling the 'seaside craze' in the latter part of the 18th century. This, combined with changing social norms, contributed to the emergence of coastal resorts such as Brighton and Scarborough. Few medical experts questioned the therapeutic benefits of seawater, despite their doubts.

By the mid-1800s, when mandatory leave for senior male staff came into play in the UK, and the idea of outdoor swimming and the consumption of or exposure to seawater for its health benefits had become more firmly rooted, the railway provided easier access to what became booming coastal resorts. In time, the resorts developed to accommodate people's desire for entertainment and amenities: piers, pavilions, lengthy promenades, bathing boxes (segregated by gender) and children's entertainment were set up to draw people to Britain's beaches, together with cafés, restaurants and curiosities. No longer were recreational activities for the upper classes alone – they became more accessible and acceptable. Towns sprang up around the resorts. The National Swimming Society was founded in 1837 and began to organise outdoor swimming events and teach swimming techniques.

Concurrently, in France, the first commercial gymnasium was opened by Hippolyte Triat in the 1830s, and by 1847 he had opened a popular gymnasium in Paris, which was a cultural centre of influence across Europe. The foundation for health improvement, body sculpting and the pursuit of wellness became well established.

In Britain, Edwardian and Victorian women had poorer facilities available to them. The austere laws and recommendations regarding acceptable bathing apparel reflected fundamental gender divides, despite the popularity of the sport and the recommendation of doctors of the health benefits of swimming for women.

In South Africa, coastal resorts were largely 20th-century developments. It is true that rocky coves were closed in informally, and that fishing traps or whaling pools were used for bathing purposes, but from 1910–1939 the Cape coast experienced significant municipal investment, and not inconsiderable private investment. However, the advent of World War II severely curtailed the spending.

From 1910, the development of the railways helped to expedite the development of the coastal resorts of the Cape and popularise places like St James, Kalk Bay and Muizenberg (referred to as the 'Brighton of the Cape' in tourism guides around that time). The randlords, seeking relief from the heat of the interior of the country, and having amassed vast fortunes thanks to the discovery of gold and diamonds, invested in properties along the coast.

A brief history of open-water swimming in South Africa

The history of open-water swimming in South Africa is complex, marked by racial segregation and apartheid policies that restricted access to beaches for people of colour.

For clarification, here is a timeline highlighting key milestones and events related to open-water swimming in South Africa, including the closure of some specific beaches.

1800s: Early beginnings

- **Mid-19th century:** Open-water swimming becomes a very popular recreational activity among European colonists and visitors to the Cape Colony, with many taking advantage of the country's extensive coastline. Following various health trends in Europe and Britain, sea swimming becomes a popular recreational pastime for those living at the Cape.

Early 20th century: Racial segregation

- **1913:** The Natives Land Act is passed, which limits land ownership and access to certain areas such as beaches and swimming areas for South Africa's 'non-white' population.
- **Early 1920s:** Racial segregation policies are implemented at many public facilities, including beaches and swimming pools, with separate facilities designated for different racial groups.

Apartheid era: Continued segregation

- **1948:** The National Party comes to power and formally establishes apartheid, institutionalising racial segregation and discrimination.
- **1950s–1960s:** Apartheid policies intensify, further restricting 'non-white' South Africans' access to beaches and swimming areas.

End of apartheid: Reintegration

- **1980s–1990s:** With the end of apartheid in the late 1980s and early 1990s, South Africa begins the process of dismantling segregation policies.
- **1994:** South Africa holds its first democratic elections, and Nelson Mandela becomes the country's first black president.

Present day: Progress and equality

- Since the fall of apartheid, South Africa has made significant progress in promoting racial equality.
- All of the region's once-segregated beaches, such as Strand, have been integrated, allowing people of all races to enjoy them freely.

The inspiration for the development of resorts on the Cape Peninsula can be traced back to 19th-century English coastal resorts, which served as a model for their South African counterparts. These resorts featured several essential components: railway accessibility, accommodation options, piers, entertainment pavilions, promenades and horse-drawn bathing huts along the shoreline. As time passed, additional amenities, such as donkey rides and tearooms, were introduced to enhance the overall visitor experience.

The allure of these resorts grew significantly when they became favoured destinations for royalty and celebrities. The Marine Hotel and adjacent Marine Pool in Hermanus serve as prime examples: renowned authors and nobility visited here, among them Nicholas Monsarrat and Queen Victoria's granddaughter HRH Princess Alice, adding a touch of glamour to the hotel's enduring success and appeal.

Development efforts were happening concurrently along both the Atlantic and False Bay coastlines. Notable developments along the Atlantic included a privately constructed pool and pavilion at Sea Point (1895), a swimming pool and pavilion at Camps Bay (1904), the Adderley Street Pier in 1913, and the pavilion at Woodstock in 1914.

The construction of tidal pools along the Cape Peninsula coastline began in the late 1890s, with the first one established by a private company in a rocky inlet at Sea Point. More tidal pools were subsequently built along the rugged stretches of this coastline, reaching as far as Camps Bay. As the 20th century progressed and Cape Town expanded, tidal pools also emerged along the False Bay coast, extending from St James to Kalk Bay. In the 1930s, further expansion occurred southward, with the addition of tidal pools at Glencairn, followed by pools at Buffels Bay within the Cape of Good Hope Nature Reserve (now Cape Point Nature Reserve) and Miller's Point in the 1960s.

The creation of these tidal pools was motivated by various factors, including the popularity of sea bathing, its purported health benefits and the enduring influence of English culture on the Cape's customs. Weather conditions also played a role, bearing in mind the Cape's designation as the 'Cape of Storms' by early settlers. The storms and harsh winters of the region likely contributed to the desire to establish safer swimming spots along the scenic coastline.

During apartheid, millions of people were banned from many of the stunning areas in the Western Cape. White residents were granted most coastal access, particularly in prime locations often bordering smaller areas designated for 'coloured' residents, as seen in places like Hout Bay and Muizenberg.

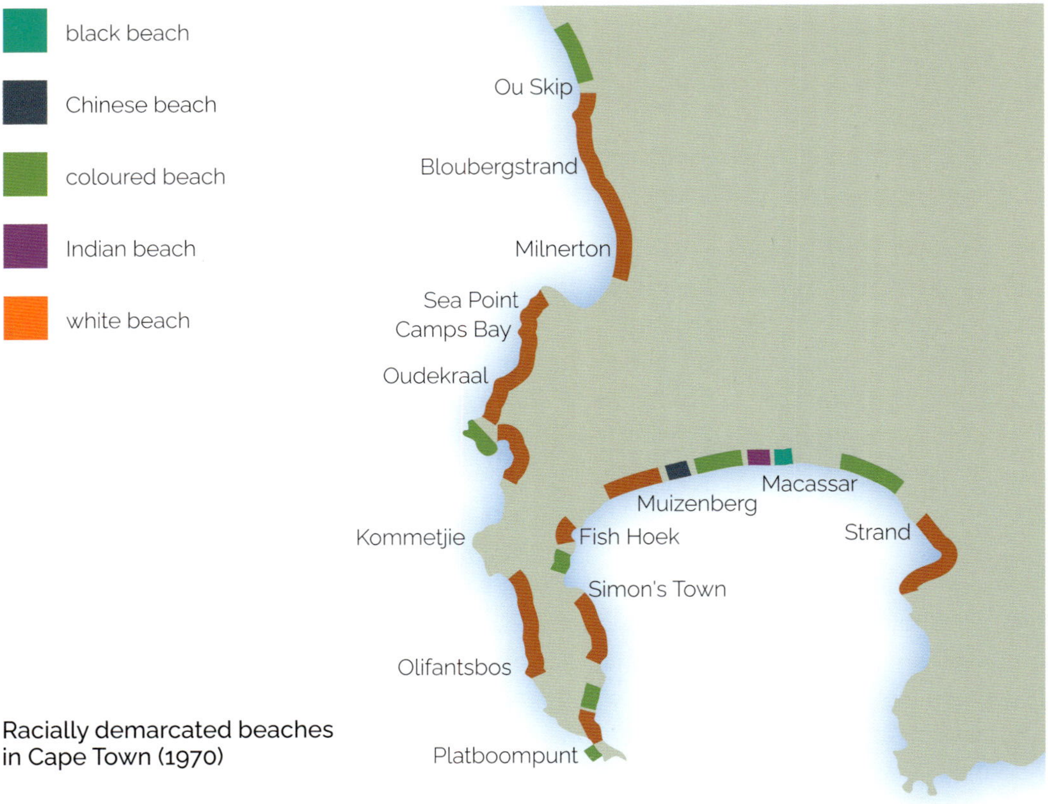

Racially demarcated beaches in Cape Town (1970)

Jayne Rogerson writes about the clear favouring of some racial groups in 'Kicking Sand in the Face of Apartheid':

> In Cape Town national government representatives were only prepared to concede minimal beach space for use by Coloureds in the Cape Peninsula at a distance of 21 miles from the city centre and at an outlying beach to which no public transport was available (Sunday Times 22 March 1964). In addition it was reported several Coloured beach spaces were not only difficult to access but were 'dangerous in terms of swimming and bathing' (Horrell, 1967). The unequal allocation of beach facilities for different race groups is well illustrated by the area of Simonstown … In Simonstown where 61% of the local population was non-white the best beaches and amenities were allocated for the exclusive use of white bathers.

The more liberal of the City of Cape Town authorities were against demarcating segregated beaches. In 1965, however, as Roger Omond notes in *The Apartheid Handbook*, those beaches that were open to 'non-white' people were 'found to be considerable distances from their homes, lacking in amenities and sometimes dangerous'. The council refused to put up no-entry signs until instructed to do so by the National Party–controlled administration. In the 1970s, apartheid architecture was in full effect. As Durrheim and Dixon comment, '[T]he Sea Shore Amendment Act (1972) empowered the Minister of Agriculture to confer control

of the beaches to local and provincial authorities'. Subsequently, the central government persisted in exerting political influence on local authorities, urging them to rigorously implement segregation policies at beaches.

In 1978, the Cape Administrator made the decision to dedicate provincial government funds solely to the improvement of beaches open to everyone. By 1985, Cape Town had commenced the process of unifying its beaches.

During the 1980s, as apartheid faced mounting pressure and began to deteriorate, Cape Town experienced relatively minimal resistance to integrated beaches compared to cities like Port Elizabeth or Durban. In the politically liberal climate of 1980s Cape Town, public sentiment towards beach segregation took a notable shift. Rather than focusing solely on the reopening of beaches, local discussions turned towards vehement opposition to the exclusionary measures enforced by authorities. The controversial topic centred around the local government's actions to fence off beaches and impose access fees on what were paradoxically labelled as 'open beaches', effectively making them inaccessible to people of colour.

Amid the escalating anti-apartheid movement, South Africa's beaches transformed into settings for nonviolent defiance. Activists orchestrated a range of initiatives – from protest swims to multiracial gatherings dubbed 'unity dips' – at beaches restricted to whites. Led by the Mass Democratic Movement, which united various communities, campaigns emerged with rallying cries such as 'Break the Chains of Beach Apartheid' and 'Equal Access to Our Coastlines'. These endeavours encompassed protest gatherings and synchronised actions to claim access to beaches historically reserved for whites only.

The desegregation of beaches wasn't an isolated incident; rather, it unfolded within the broader context of the demise of the apartheid regime. In 1986, Cape Town took the initiative to open all its beaches without seeking approval from local authorities. By 1989, free access to beaches was established across much of the Cape Peninsula. In November of that year, State President F.W. de Klerk called upon local authorities to desegregate any remaining beaches designated for specific racial groups, resulting in the opening of all beaches by the end of 1989.

South Africa's history of segregation and apartheid in particular had a profound impact on access to public spaces, including beaches, for people of colour. The struggle for equal access to these spaces is an important part of the country's history. In this context, we can better understand how and why tidal pools can play a vital role in a newly 'integrated' society. This extends well beyond health benefits and offering safe swimming spaces into creating the opportunity for regular social connection, respite and meaningful inclusivity.

Open-water swimming

Getting started

Sea temperature

The sea temperature impacts the water temperature in each pool. Water that has been standing, without fresh seawater feeding it, can have a higher temperature than a pool with more frequent fresh seawater entering it. Heavy rains and prolonged winds can influence the temperature of the water. In the Western Cape, sea temperatures don't vary greatly between summer and winter, which makes all-year-round swimming perfectly possible. The best months for swimming in warmer temperature waters are January, February, March, October and December.

Average water temperatures:
Spring 16.7°C | Summer 20.4°C | Autumn 18.6°C | Winter 16°C

Source: https://seatemperature.net/current/south-africa/cape-town-western-cape-south-africa-sea-temperature

Gear

While swimming in tidal pools isn't quite open-water swimming, much of the same gear should be used and the same safety advice followed (a list of recommended gear is included on page 185). To some extent, the quality of your experience will be influenced by the gear you have with you. You'll see locals wearing anything from their underwear to head-to-toe 8-mm wetsuits and booties!

Basic gear includes a bathing suit (none of the featured pools allows nudity), towel, swimming cap if the water is particularly cold and you're planning a good few lengths, water shoes/booties to avoid injury if you step on an urchin, a wetsuit if colder water really isn't your cup of tea, earplugs for the water babies among us, and goggles. Reflective goggles help keep the sun out of your eyes and allow you to enjoy the beauty of the marine life of the pool.

Safety

Swimming in colder water requires a level of awareness not only of your own personal comfort levels in order to prevent hypothermia, but also of signs of drowning in other bathers. While the dangers are fairly minimal and often barely worth thinking about, caution prevents serious harm and injury.

Hypothermia, a dangerous drop in body temperature, exhibits several key signs. Initial symptoms include shivering, confusion and numbness in extremities. As it progresses, speech may become slurred and coordination impaired, and shivering could cease. Severe

Wild swimming next to the demolished Graaff's Pool

cases lead to disorientation, slowed heart rate and unconsciousness. Swift medical attention is crucial if hypothermia is suspected.

Drowning can be silent and swift. Watch for struggling swimmers tilting their head back, gasping or trying to roll onto their back. Their arms may move downward, and their body may remain upright. Children might bob in the water or exhibit a glassy-eyed stare. If these signs are present, act immediately to prevent drowning.

It's a good idea to keep a first-aid kit in your car or beach bag for unforeseen circumstances. An important item to include is tweezers to remove pesky urchin quills if you're unlucky enough to stand on one. There is a list of essential first-aid kit items on page 187.

While the 34 pools chosen for this book are extremely beautiful, some of them are less safe than others, as crime is a sad reality in South Africa. The rule of thumb is always to swim in groups, and visit the pools at the most popular times of day (around 6.30 a.m. to 9 a.m. and 5.30 p.m. to 7 p.m.). Be aware of shady characters lurking and place your possessions where you can see them.

Spring and neap tides

Spring tides and neap tides are two distinct phases of the ocean's tidal cycle, influenced by the gravitational interactions between the earth, the moon and the sun.

Spring tides occur during the new moon and full moon phases when the earth, moon and sun align. During spring tides, the gravitational pull of the moon and the sun combines, leading to the highest high tides and the lowest low tides. This results in a more significant difference between high and low tides, and it is when the sea level reaches its extremes. Spring high tides usually begin a day before a full or new moon and continue for one or two days after. During spring tides the high tide will fall between 2.30 and 4.30 both a.m. and p.m. There are about six hours between high tide and low tide.

Neap tides, on the other hand, happen during the first and third quarters of the moon when the gravitational forces of the moon and sun are at right angles to each other. As a result, their combined influence is weakened, resulting in milder high and low tides. The difference between high and low tides during neap tides is less pronounced than during spring tides.

Check the tide schedule before you go and be mindful of changing conditions, such as currents and weather.

Lifeguards

During the summer months there are lifeguards on duty at the busier tidal pools, but not all of them. In winter there are no lifeguards on duty at all.

Kalk Bay Tidal Pools on a summer day

Dog friendly

Unfortunately, dogs are not allowed at any tidal pool, whether on or off the leash, as per the rules of the City of Cape Town. If rules change, the City of Cape Town releases a new guide to dog-friendly beaches and tidal pools.

The blue and cold: Health benefits of cold-water swimming

Swimming in cold water, also known as cold-water immersion, has been studied for its potential health benefits, particularly when practised safely and responsibly. Here are some scientifically proven benefits of swimming in cold water.

Improved circulation

Cold-water immersion can cause vasoconstriction (narrowing of blood vessels), which may help improve circulation and increase blood flow to vital organs and muscles.

Enhanced immune function

Some studies suggest that regular exposure to cold water may stimulate the immune system, potentially leading to an increased production of white blood cells and other immune responses.

Mental health benefits

Cold-water swimming is associated with a release of endorphins and other 'feel-good' neurotransmitters, which can lead to improved mood and reduced stress and anxiety.

Calorie burning and weight management

Exposure to cold water requires the body to work harder to maintain its core temperature, which can lead to increased energy expenditure and potentially contribute to weight management.

Reduced inflammation

Immersion in cold water may help reduce inflammation in the body, which is associated with various chronic conditions.

Pain relief

Cold-water exposure has been shown to have analgesic effects, potentially reducing pain and improving muscle recovery after exercise.

Skin health

Swimming in cold water can promote healthy skin by improving blood circulation to the skin's surface and potentially enhancing skin elasticity.

Improved respiratory health

Exposure to cold water may enhance lung function and improve respiratory health by training the body to adapt to different breathing patterns.

Stress adaptation

Repeated exposure to cold water can help the body adapt to stressors and improve overall resilience.

Mental toughness and mindfulness

Cold-water swimming requires mental focus and can help build mental toughness, mindfulness and a sense of accomplishment.

It's important to note that while there are benefits to cold-water immersion, there are also potential risks involved, especially if not done safely. Cold-water exposure can lead to hypothermia, shock and other adverse effects if precautions are not taken. People with serious medical conditions, such as heart problems, epilepsy, hypertension, circulatory diseases, renal conditions and mental health conditions (including anxiety), and people taking beta blockers or antipsychotics should consult a healthcare professional before engaging in cold-water swimming.

Swimming in cold water should always be approached with caution and proper preparation. Gradually acclimate to colder water, never swim alone and ensure that you are aware of the potential risks and safety measures.

The benefits of tidal pools for mental health

According to the *Lancet*, poor mental health is projected to cost the global economy $6 trillion annually by 2030. More than 80% of the global mental health burden occurs in low- and middle-income countries.

While South Africa may not be categorised as a post-conflict zone akin to Liberia and Sierra Leone, its history is marked by brutality, sustained adversity and dehumanisation. Despite its democratic status, the societal scars of the past persist. According to a 2021 report on the mental state of world, South Africa ranks among the worst countries for mental health.

The healthcare system is severely underfunded, with only 4% of the national health budget allocated to mental health treatment. Research released in the Child Gauge shows that children who experience multidimensional poverty, such as in South Africa's poorest communities, experience toxic stress at pandemic levels. New research from local adolescent mental health organisations shows that social connectedness, safe outdoor spaces and learning a new skill act as mental health prevention/promotion tools for at-risk adolescents. Population growth in urban areas places public services under strain, and in an already resource-constrained city we need to think carefully about how we maintain safe outdoor spaces such as tidal pools.

In light of the mental health challenges for both adults and adolescents in a society struggling to keep its head above water, safe shared outdoor spaces emerge as vital resources. They provide a welcome opportunity for children and adults to access the healing power of nature. Preserving and supporting these spaces is becoming increasingly crucial in addressing mental health challenges in the South African context.

Tidal pools offer a wealth of benefits. They provide a secure environment for swimming, with their shallow, sheltered waters away from turbulent waves. Moreover, they are easily accessible and generally safe. Immerse yourself in the beauty of green and blue spaces, finding solace from stress and enjoying the peace they offer. Swimming not only provides physical activity but also demands full presence, diverting attention from mental stress. Research from Wallace Nichols, noted in his seminal book *Blue Mind*, recognises that water induces a calm, meditative state, which he termed the 'Blue Mind state'. It isn't too big a leap to understand how tidal pools can support our experience of the Blue Mind state and how beneficial this can be to treat stress and anxiety.

Tidal pools also create opportunities for connection, whether through swim groups, making new friends or challenging yourself to explore beyond the ordinary. Engaging in group activities fosters positive peer interactions and friendships, contributing to self-care. As we swim, our breathing naturally slows, and the rhythmic nature of swimming often unconsciously teaches us self-regulation techniques.

Many find solace in shedding the stresses of the day or creating moments of joy before work by visiting a pool and connecting with friends. It's a quest to truly embrace our one wild and precious life, and make each day count.

Tidal pools have the potential to be reframed not just as spaces for leisure activity but also as a space that supports community mental health. We understand how essential tidal pools are for ocean conservation, but we may only be beginning to understand the potential for their impact on community mental health and well-being.

Unfortunately, for many of Cape Town's underserved populations, visiting tidal pools can be costly and challenging owing to a lack of safe or accessible transport, both public and private. This remains a challenge associated with apartheid geography and how its remnants continue to negatively impact those who, arguably, are most in need of low-cost, safe outdoor spaces.

Six ways blue spaces support mental health

Stress reduction

Spending time in natural environments has been linked to a reduction in stress levels. Exposure to green and blue spaces can lower cortisol (a stress hormone) levels, leading to increased relaxation and a sense of calm.

Improved mood

Being in natural settings can enhance one's mood and reduce symptoms of anxiety and depression. Nature experiences are associated with increased feelings of happiness and well-being.

Enhanced cognitive function

Exposure to green spaces has been linked to improved cognitive function, including better attention and concentration. This can have a positive impact on overall mental well-being.

Social interaction

Green spaces provide opportunities for social interaction and community engagement, which can reduce feelings of loneliness and promote a sense of belonging. Social support is vital for mental health.

Restoration and stress recovery

Natural settings afford opportunities for mental restoration and stress recovery, helping people recover from mental fatigue and emotional strain.

Sense of connection

Being in green and blue spaces fosters a sense of connection to the natural world, which can promote a sense of purpose and meaning in life, contributing to overall mental well-being.

An overview of the marine life of the pools

One Cape, two coasts

Sandwiched between the Indian Ocean to the east and the Atlantic Ocean to the west, Cape Point on the southernmost tip of the Cape Peninsula marks the divide between the southern and western coasts of South Africa. Sea life differs on either side of the Cape Peninsula owing to the differences in temperature and nutrition, and the changes in wave frequency and velocity.

On the southern coast (from Cape Point eastwards) the Agulhas Current brings warm water from the tropics, while on the West Coast (from Cape Point north and west) the Benguela Current brings icy water from the Antarctic. The southern coast differs geologically too, with softer calcrete banks and shelly beaches, while the West Coast has harder sandstone shelves with softer white beaches. Tempestuous waves hitting the coast coupled with the colder, highly nutritious waters of the Benguela result in an abundance of vast kelp forests, which harbour a rich diversity of sea life.

This is an area of extreme variability: swell size can remain large or small for weeks at a time or change drastically in a 24-hour period. Winds can pick up suddenly, blowing surface water in a particular direction, which can lower the temperature on one side of the peninsula by a few degrees while raising it on the other side. The fortnightly spring tides can make a significant difference, especially at the more steeply inclined parts of the coast.

The creatures that live in the intertidal zones of the Western Cape have evolved to be adapted for extreme change. I've included a list of recommended reading at the end of the book for those who wish to deepen their knowledge of the marine life of South Africa's shores.

Important note: It is a crime to remove any form of marine life from tidal pools; however, with a licence, which can be purchased from post offices, you may collect some species from surrounding rock pools in certain areas.

Here are a few of the most common forms of marine life near the tidal pools:

- **Algae** are a diverse group of aquatic organisms that can range from microscopic single-celled organisms to large multicellular forms. Representing the plant world of the sea, algae (along with seaweeds) are an integral part of the intertidal ecosystem and form the base of the food pyramid, with many of the creatures here feeding directly on the living plant or on dead plants' decomposing matter. Algae can be classified into several groups based on their pigmentation, such as green, red and brown algae.

- **Anemones**, though named after an earthly flower, are carnivorous, mobile sea creatures related to jellyfish. They sit anchored to rocks waiting for their prey to come within reach of their tentacles. There are hundreds of types of anemone and their prey is varied, ranging from small crabs and molluscs to small fish. They are, in general, harmless to humans and come in a host of beautiful shapes and colours.

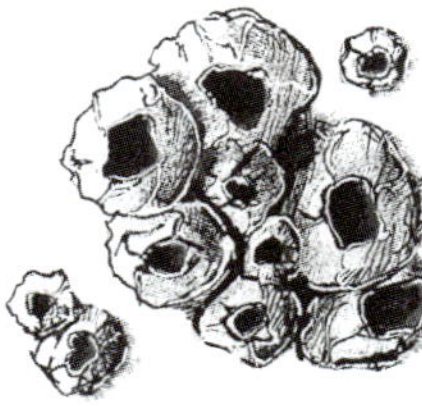

- **Barnacles** are cousins of the crab, who choose their neighbourhood and never move. They see out their days filtering the incoming and outgoing tides by sticking their feathery limbs out of their crater-like doors and hiding out in their hard, spiky houses.

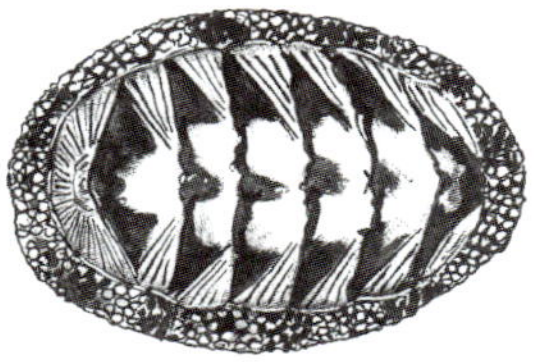

- **Chitons** are hard-shelled creatures with eight overlapping plates stuck tightly to the rock. If you look carefully at the bottom of rock pools you may spot them, well camouflaged and elusive. Though very slow, these creatures are mobile and cruise the intertidal zone for good algal grazing.

- **Crabs** are members of the ten-legged (decapod) crustacean family, and small varieties inhabit the Western Cape rock pools. They are largely omnivorous, feeding mostly on algae but also on other small invertebrates.

- **Feather-duster worms or sabellidae** look like nondescript pipes attached to the rock. When they are undisturbed, feather-like limbs protrude from the mouth of the pipe to filter the water for food. As soon as one touches them or gets too close, the limbs disappear back into their pipe home.

- **Klipvissies (rockfish)** consist of a few different species of Clinidae. They can be seen in the rock pools darting for cover as children approach with their nets. Beautifully patterned and quite small, they are found mainly in rock pools, where they live out their entire life cycle. Eggs are laid in the submerged seaweed and often guarded by the adult. They feed on whatever crustaceans or molluscs they can catch.

- **Limpets** are – like snails, whelks and periwinkles – gastropods, which means 'stomach-foot'. Their rough triangular, star-like shells are seen all over the intertidal zone, gripping tightly to the rocks, almost impossible to remove by hand. Limpets do, however, move about, scraping algae off the rocks with their crystalline teeth, which they make from the iron in the rocks.

- **Mussels** are seen in their thousands attached to the rocks in great banks of black and blue. They are bivalve molluscs that filter-feed on microscopic nutritious animals that wash over their shells.

- **Nudibranchs** are beautiful relations of the snail; however, these gastropod molluscs do not have shells. Instead, they gracefully swim about in the nude, dazzling everyone with their beautiful colours and sultry movements, on the hunt for less mobile prey.

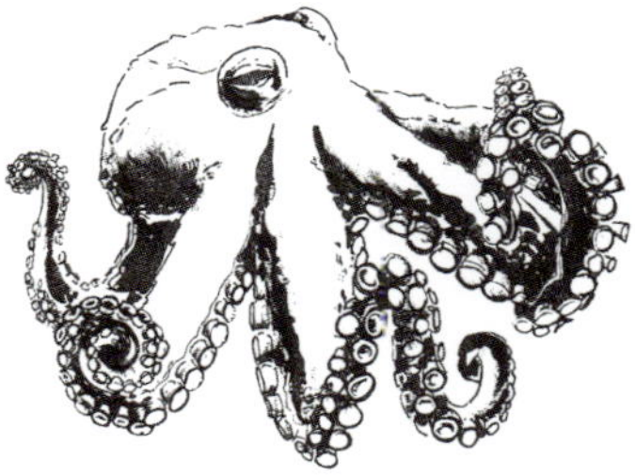

- **Octopuses** are intelligent and so adept at camouflage that they are rarely seen. Related to squids and nautili, octopuses are carnivorous cephalopods ('head-foot') that hunt larger animals such as crabs, crayfish and other molluscs. They have been known to keep gardens and recognise individuals. A special visitor to any rock pool.

- **Periwinkles** range from tiny black pinheads to about the size of a ping-pong ball. These darkly coloured sea snails are ubiquitous around the southern African coast, along with limpets and mussels, though they would certainly win any race for speed. They are mainly herbivorous, using their toothy tongues, known as a radula, to lick rocks for algae.

- **Puffadder shysharks or 'Happy Eddies'** (from its Latin name *Haploblepharus edwardsii*) have slender bodies and markings like those of their reptilian counterpart. As the name implies, they are a shy species and roll up into a tight ball when threatened. They prefer rocky reefs and can usually be spotted in a small group. Puffadder shysharks are not a threat to humans.

Shelley Point Tidal Pool

- **Sea cucumbers** are related to the starfish. These strange creatures are relatively shy in the rock pools, sometimes only showing their star-shaped tentacles while hiding their slug-like bodies beneath the sand. They are chiefly scavengers, feeding on decaying matter.

- **Sea stars and starfish (echinoderms)** are enchanting five-limbed sea creatures with elegant shapes and sometimes bold colouring. Ranging from about the size of a thumbnail with rounded points (sea star) to larger than an adult hand with distinct arms (starfish), these omnivorous animals are mobile consumers in the pools and are keystone members of the community responsible for, among other things, removing decaying matter from the intertidal zones and regulating populations in the ecosystem.

- **Seaweeds** are found everywhere along the coastline, offering a buffer effect from waves. They also provide shelter to various animals and come in a huge variety of colours and shapes. Most seaweed is edible to humans and it's regarded by some as a culinary delicacy. As mentioned previously, a licence is required to remove any marine life from tidal pools; if harvesting seaweed, be careful only to remove what is needed and use scissors rather than ripping a whole plant from the rocks.

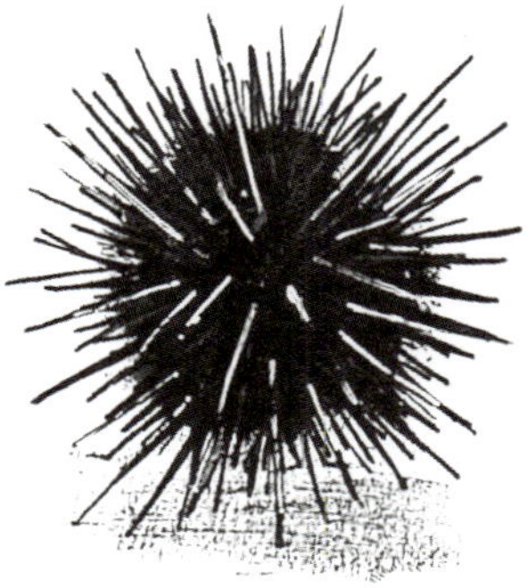

- **Urchins** were famously studied by the Ancient Greek philosopher and scientist Aristotle, who gave his name to the complicated mouth system on their undersides, which is known as Aristotle's lantern. Urchins often make for unpleasant encounters at the seaside because their barbed spines can lodge in our feet. If you gently prise one off the rocks and place it in the palm of your hand, you can watch how the spines act as legs for locomotion. Tiny suckers attach them to their positions on the rocks while they graze on algae. Their shells are often sought out by beachgoers for their beautiful radial symmetry. However, it is important to note that, according to the Marine Living Resources Act 1998, it is a crime to remove shells from the sea or the seashore unless you have a permit, which stipulates the number of shells you may remove for your own use.

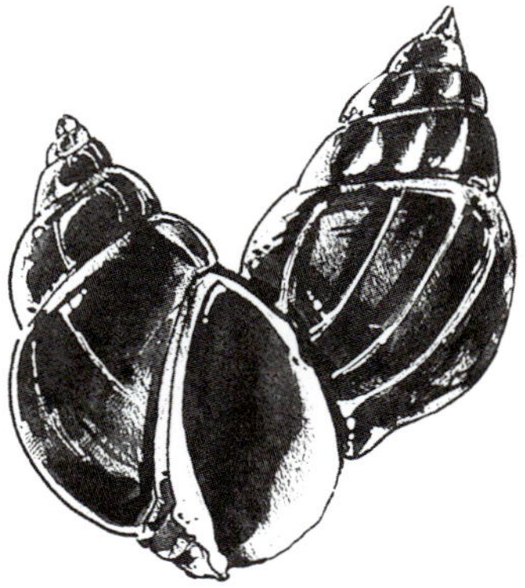

- **Whelks** are marine gastropod molluscs commonly found in coastal waters worldwide. They are carnivorous predators that primarily feed on bivalves such as clams and mussels, using their strong, drill-like radula to bore into the shells of their prey. They are known for their spiral-shaped shells, which vary in size and colour, with some species exhibiting striking patterns and hues. Whelks play a vital role in marine ecosystems as both predators and scavengers, contributing to the natural balance of coastal food webs. They are often harvested for their meat, which is considered a delicacy in various culinary traditions and is used like escargot in dishes; as mentioned before, a licence is necessary to do this.

Some of the larger animals found near tidal pools:

- **African black oystercatchers** are distinctive coastal birds native to the southern coastlines of Africa, renowned for their striking ebony plumage, contrasting bright red eyes and long crimson legs. These features make them easily identifiable along rocky shores. With a diet primarily consisting of molluscs, particularly limpets and mussels, the oystercatcher employs its strong chisel-like bill to expertly prise shells open, a remarkable adaptation for its specialised diet. Known for its strong territorial instincts, it is fiercely protective of its nest, which is usually a simple scrape in the sand or gravel, often near rocky outcrops. During the breeding season, it performs aerial displays and makes loud calls to defend its territory. This charismatic bird species is of conservation concern owing to its restricted range and vulnerability to habitat disturbance, human encroachment and climate change impacts on its coastal habitats.
- **African penguins** are the predominant penguin species in southwestern South Africa, particularly along the Western Cape coastline. Also known as the jackass penguin for their donkey-like calls, they are well adapted to the region's coastal habitats. Recognisable by their black-and-white plumage, with distinctive chest markings and pink patches around the eyes and beak, these

relatively small penguins are about 60–70 cm tall. They primarily inhabit islands and coastal areas, nesting in burrows or rocky crevices. There is a famous colony at Boulders Beach in Simon's Town. Classified as endangered, African penguins face threats such as habitat loss, prey overfishing and oil pollution; this has prompted conservation efforts to safeguard their existence and coastal habitats in South Africa. Despite how cute and harmless penguins may look, they are still wild animals and require a wide birth. Do not try to pet them.

- **Angulate tortoises** are endemic to the Western Cape. They primarily inhabit the fynbos, where they can be found foraging on succulents and grasses. They are most active during the day, basking in the sun to regulate their body temperature and retreating into the shade or underground burrows during hot weather. They are solitary creatures and are generally shy, withdrawing into their shells when threatened or approached by predators. They can be identified by their domed shell with prominent angular scutes, ranging in colour from yellowish-brown to dark brown. They are relatively small compared to other tortoise species, typically reaching lengths of around 15–20 cm.

- **Baboons** are highly adaptable primates, easily identifiable by their robust build, long muzzles and distinctive fur coloration, which ranges from olive-green to brown. They inhabit a variety of habitats including mountainous, coastal areas and semi-arid regions, often preferring areas with access to water sources and ample food supply. Opportunistic omnivores, they consume a diet that includes fruits, seeds, insects, small mammals and even food scavenged from human settlements. Their habitat preferences often intersect with human areas, leading to conflicts over food and territory. Baboons play a crucial role in their ecosystem as seed dispersers, and can significantly impact plant diversity through their foraging behaviours.

- **Bontebok** are endemic to the Cape Floral Region. These antelopes have a striking chestnut-brown coat with a white belly, face and rump, with a noticeable white blaze running down the centre of their faces. Their horns are lyre-shaped and present in both males and females, although the males' are typically thicker and longer. Bontebok prefer open grasslands and fynbos habitats, where they feed on a variety of grasses and browse on shrubs and herbs.

- **Cape clawless otters** are the world's second-largest freshwater otter species. Thriving in both freshwater and coastal environments, these otters exhibit adaptability in scavenging and hunting. Their prevalence in southern Africa is notable: they are often found near permanent bodies of water. They are visitors to tidal pools, using the pools as an extension of their hunting grounds in the sea. Unlike marine mammals, they lack a subcutaneous fat layer, relying instead on dense, chestnut-coloured fur for insulation, which they maintain through rigorous grooming. They do not have claws on their front paws, which are adapted for digging. Cape clawless otters are predators with powerful molar teeth and consume a diverse diet. Weighing 10–21 kg, with a length of up to 2 m, including their tails, they showcase both size and grace. Caution and respect are advised in interactions with these creatures, which are active at dawn and dusk.

- **Cape dune mole rats** are large rodents that dig tunnels throughout the sandy coastal plains of the province. This solitary furry creature with massive incisors can shift about half a ton of sand a month and leaves notable mounds wherever it goes. Its primary diet consists of bulbs, and its primary concern is the large mole snake that sits just above it in the food chain.

- **Cape fur seals** are characterised by the dense dark brown fur that helps them stay warm in the cold waters of the Atlantic Ocean. Several colonies can be found in the Western Cape, including on Seal Island near Hout Bay, Duiker Island near Gansbaai and Robben Island. Cape fur seals are well adapted to their marine environment and are often seen swimming, diving and basking on rocks. They mainly feed on fish and other marine prey.

- **Cape gannets** are known for their striking appearance and distinctive black eye markings. The only gannet species found in South Africa, Cape gannets have predominantly white plumage with black wingtips, a yellowish hue on their head and black markings that extend around their eyes, giving them a distinctive masked appearance. They are medium-sized seabirds, with a wingspan of approximately 1.8 m. They primarily feed on shoaling fish, notably pilchards and anchovies. Highly adapted for marine life, they dive from great heights to catch their prey. Cape gannets breed in large colonies on offshore islands such as Bird Island near Lambert's Bay and rocky outcrops along the South African coastline. Birdwatchers and nature enthusiasts often visit these colonies to observe these magnificent seabirds during their breeding season. The conservation status of Cape gannets is a matter of concern, as they face threats such as overfishing of their prey, pollution and habitat disturbance. They are noted as an endangered species.

- **Cape grysbok** are endemic to South Africa, primarily inhabiting the Cape Floral Region, where dense cover is crucial for their habitat. They are solitary and elusive, as a result of which they are seldom spotted. Unfortunately, they are targeted by poachers for bushmeat, owing to their vulnerability to snares. Cape grysbok have selective grazing habits, but are also known to consume grass as part of their diet.

- **Eland** are the largest antelopes in the Cape Point Nature reserve, characterised by their size, distinctive spiral horns and a dewlap hanging from their necks. Their coat is typically a tawny colour, sometimes with vertical white stripes on their sides. Eland are predominantly browsers, feeding on a variety of grasses, leaves and shrubs. Their habits contribute to the maintenance of the reserve's ecosystem by controlling vegetation growth and promoting plant diversity.

- **Plains zebras** are known for their black-and-white striped coats, which are unique to each individual. Zebras can often be spotted grazing in open grasslands or meandering through the scrubland habitats of the Cape Point Nature Reserve.
- Seagulls:
  - Kelp gulls are the most common seagull species in Cape Town and along the South African coastline. They are known for their striking black-and-white plumage, yellow bills and red orbital rings around their eyes. Kelp gulls are often seen scavenging for food around harbours, beaches and coastal areas.
  - Hartlaub's gulls are a smaller species, with grey wings. They are frequently spotted along the Cape Town coastline, especially around rocky shores.
  - Grey-headed gulls are less common than kelp gulls, but are occasionally seen in Cape Town and other coastal areas. They have a distinctive grey head and a white body, with black markings on their wings.

- Whales:
  - The dominant whale species that captures the attention of onlookers is the southern right whale. These magnificent marine mammals are known for their colossal size, with adults reaching lengths of more than 15 m. One of their distinguishing features is the lack of a dorsal fin on their broad, dark backs. Their immense arching mouths and callosities – rough patches of skin covered in barnacles – make them easily identifiable. During the winter months, southern right whales migrate from their feeding grounds to the warmer waters near Cape Town for breeding and calving. The sheltered bays and coastal areas, such as False Bay and Walker Bay, become vital nurseries for their calves. Visitors to these regions are often treated to awe-inspiring displays of breaching, tail-slapping and flipper-waving as the southern right whales engage in courtship rituals and caring for their newborns.

- While southern right whales dominate the scene, humpback whales and Bryde's whales are also encountered off the coast of Cape Town. Humpbacks are celebrated for their acrobatic displays, including leaping out of the water and slapping their long pectoral fins. Bryde's whales, with their streamlined bodies and subtle ridges along their heads, are known for their year-round presence in warmer waters, making them a common sight in the region. The rich marine ecosystem of Cape Town's coastal waters provides a haven for these magnificent cetaceans, offering unforgettable experiences for those fortunate enough to witness their grandeur.

- White-fronted sandplovers are small shorebirds partial to sandy beaches, dunes and mudflats. Interestingly, this species is monogamous and has a life expectancy of 12 years. Adult male plovers have a white patch on their forehead and above their eyes, with a dark stripe across the tip of their head. The rest of their head is mostly white, with a dark brown stripe from their eye to their ear. Their upper body is light brownish-grey, with some feathers having pale edges. The tail feathers are mostly black and white. Their wings are dark brown with white markings. They have a light brown patch on their chest and white belly. Their eyes are brown, their bill is black, and their legs can be pale grey or greenish-grey.

Spiny sea star *(Marthasterias africana)* found at St James Tidal Pool

Pools in intertidal zones: Sanctuaries and nurseries

On our coastline, safe waters are crucial havens for delicate parts of the ecosystem. Both natural and man-made pools provide homes for various creatures to flourish. These waters are calmer than the open sea and not as deep, making them warmer and full of decomposing matter that supports life.

They are also safe from larger predators and provide perfect breeding conditions for a wealth of organisms. This serves the broader environment by creating biodiversity at the lower levels of the food pyramid, a rich source of food for the larger marine species.

An added bonus is that these pools create the space for humans to interact with and learn from the marine environment in a safe and fun way. Visits to pools like these along our coast have given early inspiration to many a young marine biologist or conservationist.

An excellent example of meaningful private and public partnerships can be evidenced by the methods of cleaning tidal pools. In the recent past harmful chemicals were used, a method that was challenged by a group of concerned citizens who petitioned for a more sensitive approach. In 2017 the city piloted cleaning five of the pools in an eco-friendly way and in 2020 the City of Cape Town pledged to only use an eco-friendly protocol, namely: high-pressure hoses to clean the pools, steps and walls, draining the pools only when strictly necessary, and moving animals out of harm's way, all contributing towards the conservation of these intricate and delicate ecosystems.

Marine Protected Areas

A Marine Protected Area (MPA) is a designated area within the ocean or coastal waters that is set aside for the conservation and protection of marine ecosystems, species and habitats. Regulations and restrictions placed on human activities within the boundaries of MPAs aim to eliminate or minimise harmful impacts on the marine environment. These protected areas vary in size and may include a wide range of marine habitats such as coral reefs, seagrass beds, kelp forests and open ocean environments.

MPAs provide a haven for marine species and ecosystems, allowing them to thrive without the pressures of human activities, including overfishing, habitat destruction and pollution. This helps preserve biodiversity and maintains healthy populations of marine species.

Many species rely on specific habitats for breeding, feeding and shelter, for example coral reefs, seagrass beds and estuaries. MPAs safeguard these habitats, which are essential for the survival of numerous marine organisms.

The importance of pools in the intertidal zones

Biodiversity hotspots

Tidal pools are biodiversity hotspots, serving as nurseries for various marine species and providing a haven for young fish and invertebrates to grow and develop without the threat of predators from deeper waters.

Species adaptation

The pools are microcosms of marine life where species have adapted to extreme fluctuations in environmental conditions, including temperature, salinity and exposure to air during low tide. This adaptation showcases the resilience of life in the intertidal zone.

Ecosystem services

Tidal pools contribute to the overall health of the coastal environment. They act as natural filters, helping to maintain water quality by removing excess nutrients and pollutants. Their biodiversity also supports local fisheries by providing a source of food for larger species.

Educational and recreational value

Beyond their ecological importance, tidal pools offer educational opportunities for visitors and researchers. They provide a unique setting for studying marine ecology, and they offer a serene and captivating environment for beachgoers and nature enthusiasts.

Environmental challenges of the coastal zone

The Western Cape Coastline stretches for 400 km and boasts a diverse range of attractions for residents, tourists and visitors. However, this picturesque coastline is not immune to serious environmental challenges. Its intricate and interconnected natural systems, composed of estuaries, wetlands, rocky shores and sandy beaches, face threats from overuse and degradation.

Most of the residents of the Western Cape live within 25 km of the coast. Pollution, poor water quality, biodiversity loss and habitat modification are among the interconnected issues that plague the area. As a result, coastal management efforts are increasingly strained in their attempts to address these complex challenges.

One significant contributor to environmental degradation is poor waste sanitation, which leads to pollution of the marine environment. This pollution not only harms marine life but also poses serious health risks to humans. Alarmingly, of the country's effluent that is discharged into marine environments, 32% is discharged in the Western Cape, which exacerbates the situation. The challenges facing the region are compounded by the intermittent electricity supply, further straining resources and inhibiting waste management practices. As a consequence, some tidal pool have been periodically closed owing to poor water quality, which shines a spotlight on the urgency of addressing these issues.

Simple things we can do to conserve marine ecosystems

1. Implement sustainable waste management practices at home to reduce pollution levels in marine environments. These include minimising single-use plastics, recycling and properly disposing of waste.
2. At the pools, pick up plastic and leave nothing behind. Support coastal clean-ups and local organisations that lead research into how we can better protect marine ecosystems.
3. Support organisations that preserve and restore coastal habitats and biodiversity.
4. Avoid littering and use eco-friendly products.
5. Advocate for stronger regulations to protect coastal zones and promote sustainable development practices.

Venus Pool, Cape Point

Tidal pools at a glance

Best for dips

Glencairn Tidal Pool, Glencairn
Dalebrook Tidal Pool, Kalk Bay
Maiden's Cove 2, Clifton
Skellies Pool, Fish Hoek
Woolley's Tidal Pool, Kalk Bay
Jan Rabie Tidal Pool, Onrus
Ficks Pool, Hermanus

Best for training swims

Camps Bay Tidal Pool, Camps Bay
Miller's Point Tidal Pool, Simon's Town
Buffels Bay Tidal Pool, Cape Point
Kalk Bay Tidal Pools 1 & 2, Kalk Bay
Silwerstroom Tidal Pool, Silwerstroom

Best marine life

Venus Pool, Cape Point
Marine Pool, Hermanus
Sonop Sononder, Hermanus

Best for families

Glencairn Tidal Pool, Glencairn
Dalebrook Tidal Pool, Kalk Bay
Harmony Park Tidal Pool, Gordon's Bay
Camps Bay Tidal Pool, Camps Bay
Kleinbaai Tidal Pool, Kleinbaai

Best for picnics

Silwerstroom Tidal Pool, Silwerstroom
Camps Bay Tidal Pool, Camps Bay
Glencairn Tidal Pool, Glencairn
Saunders Rock Tidal Pool, Sea Point
(best for romantic picnics)
Shelley Point Tidal Pool, Glencairn
Sparks Tidal Pool, Gordon's Bay
Jan Rabie Tidal Pool, Onrus

Kalk Bay Tidal Pools just after sunrise in summer

Tidal pool hops

Tidal pool hops are swims in clusters of tidal pools done one after the other in a short period of time, such as a morning. Pools that are located close together are popular destinations for groups of people celebrating birthdays and other special events. This section describes the most popular tidal pool hops.

If you've got two to four hours, these pools are perfect for a hop, as they lie along the same stretch of coast and are relatively close.

False Bay

Dalebrook ▸ Kalk Bay 1 & 2 ▸ Woolley's

This tidal pool hop is best started early, at sunrise. Be sure to buy an almond croissant and coffee at Chardonnay Deli, then cross the road to Dalebrook Tidal Pool. After your dip, walk southwest (towards Fish Hoek) along Main Road to Kalk Bay 1 & 2, which are accessed via the subway sandwiched between some clothing stores. Once you've enjoyed a swim in these gorgeous pools, continue in the same along Main Road; do stop at Olympia Café for a stuffed croissant or fresh pastry before walking the short distance to Woolley's Tidal Pool. At this last pool enjoy the view of Fish Hoek and the bay and maybe, if the sea is flat and glassy, explore the kelp forest just off the rocks near the pool.

Skellies ▸ Glencairn ▸ Shelley Point ▸ Miller's Point

Stroll along Jager's Walk from Fish Hoek Beach to the little dipping pool called Skellies, or park on Main Road just next to the bridge over the railway line. Walk over the Sunny Cove station bridge and turn left. Skellies is about 200 m down the catwalk. After this dip, which is best accompanied by fresh coffee, jump in the car to drive the short distance to Glencairn. You can park at the beach and walk to the tidal pool; then follow the dirt track about 400 m to Shelley Point, a neglected but gorgeous little pool. Make your way back to your car and head south, but be sure to stop at the Simon's Town patisserie the Sweetest Thing for a mini-quiche; then drive through the town towards Cape Point. Take the first left turn after the Black Marlin restaurant and park. Make your way around the koppie to the Miller's Point Tidal Pool. The view across the bay to Rooiels and Hangklip can be breathtaking.

Strandfontein Tidal Pool on a Sunday morning in autumn

Cape Point Nature Reserve

Venus Pool ▸ Bordjiesrif ▸ Buffels Bay

Venus Pool is an excellent breakfast spot but get there early in summer … it can be quite busy because the sea life is so spectacular and varied, and the reserve so safe. Return to your vehicle and drive to Bordjiesrif Tidal Pool, which is great for a picnic, but look out for the baboons, which come out of nowhere to raid hampers. Your next and final pool is Buffels Bay, which is wide and deep and the perfect place to set up an umbrella for a nap on the lawn next to the pool.

If you're feeling particularly committed, start at St James Tidal Pool and have a dip at every pool from St James to Buffels Bay. This would be an all-day endeavour rather than a 'hop'.

Atlantic Ocean

Camps Bay ▸ Maiden's Cove 1 & 2 ▸ Saunders Rock

This tidal pool hop, although less popular than the Dalebrook to Woolley's hop in False Bay, is none the less just as scenic. Park anywhere along Victoria Road in Camps Bay or down one of the little side roads and make your way to the Camps Bay Tidal Pool. After a few laps, jump back into your car and head towards Clifton along Victoria Road. Just as you crest the tiny rise leaving Camps Bay, look out for a sign on your left that identifies the entrance to the parking area for Maiden's Cove. Maiden's Cove has opening and closing times on account of being an enclosed area, opening at 8 a.m. and closing at 5 p.m. Maiden's Cove 1 & 2 are some of the loveliest little pools from which to enjoy the view of the Twelve Apostles. Once you've had your fill of the gorgeous view and icy water, get back into your car and turn left out of the parking area towards Sea Point. Make your way along the coastal route until you reach a T-junction, at which point turn left. At the first circle, go straight down to the sea; at the second circle, turn left and start to look for parking – Saunders Rock is nearby. If you walk along the walkway on the sea side of the road towards Clifton, you'll come across Saunders Rock, which has clear signage. Enter the beach down some steeps steps and brave the last icy pool of this hop.

You can of course start this hop at Saunders Rock and then make your way to Camps Bay Tidal Pool but, either way, you must stop at Kleinsky's Delicatessen in Sea Point for a deluxe bagel and coffee! Kleinsky's is located closest to Saunders Rock, but not so close that you can walk to it from the tidal pool, so be sure to factor that into your trip if you feel like a pit stop on your way to or from the pool.

Saunders Rock is particularly popular and busy in the morning, so arrive early to claim a rock if you're planning to stay for breakfast.

Overberg

Davie's Pool ▶ Jan Rabie

Davie's and Jan Rabie Tidal Pools are within walking distance of each other, making this two-stop hop one that can be done more slowly, so you can take your time to savour the exquisite beauty of the area. It is recommended to take water shoes along for swimming in both these pools: the rocks around Jan Rabie are sharp, and the shifting sand at the bottom of Davie's Pool can expose the pointed edges of rock beneath.

Davie's Pool requires some GPS navigation because it isn't well signposted. You can park in the little lot that overlooks Davie's Pool and enjoy a picnic on the lawn before or after your dip, keeping in mind that there are pizza restaurants and a takeaway coffee shop near the pool.

From Davie's Pool, walk along the coastal road – there's only one – towards Vermont. Some 750 m down the road, about an eight-minute walk, you'll reach Jan Rabie Tidal Pool, which is an absolute gem. Carved into natural dark rock formations with a plentiful inflow of fresh seawater, this pool is as enticing as it is captivating. Entry to the pool can be down a gently angled walkway with handrail, or, if it's deep enough, jumping in off the side.

Jan Rabie Tidal Pool can be wild and inaccessible at high tide, so check the high and low tide times online before you start your hop.

You could leave your car at Davie's Pool and make your way back at a leisurely pace along the road, or leave another car at the parking area next to Jan Rabie Tidal Pool and drive back to Davie's Pool.

Ficks Pool ▶ Marine Pool ▶ Sonop Sononder

The only real challenge to this three-part tidal pool hop is choosing which pool to begin at. It is logical to start at one end and finish at the other, but all three pools are utterly spectacular to visit at sunrise. The views and general sense of awe and wonder which overcome one when visiting at sunrise are so impactful that one would be hard-pressed to find a better way to start the day.

Ficks Pool is well signposted from Main Road in Hermanus and also from Marine Drive, so you can't miss it. Parking can be found in a small lot just above the pool. Access to the pool is via a set of steps from the Cliff Path. Make your way across a small patch of lawn and down the steps. From the top of the steps you will see the pool, which will welcome you like a long-lost lover.

Arriving at Ficks Pool at sunrise in summer is a treat. Depending on the tide you may find a softly reflective pool containing and surrounded by marine life and animals, with waves gently breaking over the back wall, or a washing machine of wild white water with massive, crashing waves. It is recommended to visit at low to mid-tide to get the best of the pool without having to navigate death-defying feats in the morning.

The water can be icy, even in summer, so take warm clothes with you. You can leave your possessions on the rocks or concrete terraces and enter the pool from the steps, which are quite broken, or by stepping down from the rocks on the left of the pool.

Dassies scatter along the rocks and stare curiously out of their protected holes beneath bushes, perhaps wondering whether the humans braving an early-morning swim will share their breakfast with them. The pool is a marvel, and it's worth spending some time here basking on the rocks as the sun begins to warm them, before heading to Marine Pool. The restaurant at the pool does not open before 11 a.m., so if you need coffee to accompany your swim, stop at a coffee shop on your way.

Return to your car and drive towards the central hub of Hermanus along Marine Drive. Along the way you can see the Cliff Path meandering next to the rocks, then dipping from view behind bushes. As you pass the abundance of restaurants overlooking Walker Bay on your left, you'll notice the signposted Marine Hotel right in front of you. Find parking nearby and walk to the Cliff Path. As you walk along the Cliff Path towards Voëlklip and away from the restaurants, you'll soon see the large Marine Pool below. Keep to the path as it ducks and dives behind high bushes, and eventually emerge at the top of a set of steps that lead to the pool.

This pool definitely requires booties. I have yet to visit it and not come across a fellow swimmer trying to pick urchin quills from their feet!

Bring a snorkel and mask to Marine Pool – the marine life is out of this world, and so mesmerising that you may be tempted not to visit the last little pool along this hop.

The last pool is found along the Cliff Path below a sign that reads 'Sonop Sononder'. It is a little-known pool accessible only at mid- to high tide (it is too shallow at low tide). Like Venus Pool in Cape Point, it is suitable only for wallowing, owing to its diminutive size. At high tide the waves smash over the rocks, turning it into a wild area that is hard to get in and out of because the sides can be slippery. Caution is advised, but adventure is encouraged.

After your dip at Sonop Sononder, you can walk back along the Cliff Path to your car or walk up from the Cliff Path and back along the road.

34 of the region's most beautiful pools

The tidal pools

Swimmability

Under the right conditions, all the pools listed below are suitable for a dip. But for those who want to exercise more seriously, maybe front crawl for a few metres rather than bob or gently do breaststroke to the back wall, I have included a swimmability rating. For the purposes of this guide, 1 is poor for swimming lengths and 10 is excellent. The pools are listed chronologically according to the map (left), followed by the rating.

West Coast

1. Silwerstroom Tidal Pool 8

Atlantic Seaboard

2. Graaff's Pool 1
3. Milton Tidal Pool 2
4. Saunders Rock Tidal Pool 1

MAIDEN'S COVE TIDAL POOLS

5. Maiden's Cove 1 1
6. Maiden's Cove 2 5
7. Camps Bay Tidal Pool 10

Kommetjie/Slangkop

8. Die Kom Tidal Pool .... 6 at high tide

SOETWATER TIDAL POOLS

9. Soetwater 1 5
10. Soetwater 2 5

Cape Point Nature Reserve

11. Buffels Bay Tidal Pool 6
12. Bordjiesrif Tidal Pool 4
13. Venus Pool 3

False Bay

14. Miller's Point Tidal Pool 10
15. Shelley Point Tidal Pool 2
16. Glencairn Tidal Pool 3
17. Skellies Pool 2
18. Woolley's Tidal Pool 3

KALK BAY TIDAL POOLS

19. Kalk Bay 1 8
20. Kalk Bay 2 8
21. Dalebrook Tidal Pool 4
22. St James Tidal Pool 5
23. Strandfontein Tidal Pool 6
24. Monwabisi Tidal Pool 4
25. Strand Tidal Pool 2
26. Harmony Park Tidal Pool 9
27. Sparks Bay Tidal Pool 8

Overberg

28. Jan Rabie Tidal Pool 5
29. Davie's Pool .... 3 at high tide, otherwise 1
30. Ficks Pool 5
31. Marine Pool 5
32. Sonop Sononder Pool 1
33. Gansbaai Tidal Pool 1
34. Kleinbaai Tidal Pool 3

WEST COAST

The West Coast of the Western Cape is a 400-km-long stretch of coast that may initially appear to be an arid and inhospitable landscape. But the more time you spend here, the more you realise the extent to which flora and fauna have adapted: the array of species is quite astounding.

The West Coast Biodiversity Corridor is recognised as a biodiversity hotspot, boasting an impressive array of over 1 500 endemic species of plants, birds, mammals, reptiles and amphibians. An area of about 600 km^2, this corridor hosts a staggering 2 285 species of fynbos, showcasing the remarkable richness and diversity of this unique ecosystem.

The West Coast is a nature lover's paradise. As you leave Cape Town and the built-up urban environment, the scenery of the West Coast becomes more arid, with huge African skies and vast stretches of landscape. Two resorts each contain a large tidal pool, both of which are hugely popular in summer: Ganzekraal Tidal Pool and Silwerstroom Tidal Pool. Note that you can only visit Ganzekraal as a day visitor by prior arrangement. Long stretches of sandy white beaches reach along the coast around the tidal pools, creating opportunities for respite and wonder for those in need of a break from it all.

Silwerstroom Tidal Pool, West Coast

1 Silwerstroom Tidal Pool

Silwerstroom Tidal Pool, situated in Silwerstroomstrand on the West Coast, and only 12.5 km south of Ganzekraal Tidal Pool, is celebrated for its scenic position along the coastline. At the resort and pavilion to which Silwerstroom Tidal Pool is attached you'll need to pay a small day-visitor fee. Turn left once you're through the gate, drive towards the parking lot and park. Walk through the pavilion, and you will behold this large, beautiful pool.

The depth of this pool fluctuates, influenced by the tides and prevailing weather conditions. Typically, it has both shallow sections – ideal for leisurely wading – and deeper sections – perfect for swimming. This is an absolute favourite for training swims given the size and depth of the pool. If you look from the pavilion, there's a rocky wall that prevents you from seeing the full pool. When you walk closer and peer over the edge, you see a little natural cliff overlooking the pool. The cliff offers a scenic viewpoint with an incredible 180-degree view, but is not suitable for jumps into the enticing water below.

Terraced lawns overlook the pool but if you're wanting to loll about on the grass, get there early because the spaces available are snapped up quickly on warmer days. It's best to visit Silwerstroom pool in the morning – the southeaster often picks up later in the day, making the experience less pleasant, except, of course, for those who harbour a little inner grit.

The surrounding facility has been carefully designed to include easier accessibility to the pool for people with disabilities. A slightly less direct route allows the pool to be accessed via a wheelchair, from the parking lot, down a gentle slope and up to the small soft, sandy beach. The walkway unfortunately doesn't go into the water.

This tidal pool gets very busy at times, but its size allows for lots of people to share the space without being overwhelming. Take a walk along the wall around the pool to see the beautiful little rock pools, but take care not to topple in.

Silwerstroom is well suited to all levels of swimmers: children can play on the sandy shore and dip into the water, and more confident swimmers can swim lengths along the gentle curve of the back wall.

Things to do nearby:

- Start with a swim or leisurely morning at Silwerstroom pool. Then drive up the West Coast road (R27) to Route 27 Roosterkoek, a small roadside takeaway café, which is easily identified by a large Puma sign outside. Try the fresh roosterkoek (grilled bread) with a wide selection of fillings for lunch (and maybe one or two as takeaways).
- Alternatively, continue up the R27 to !Khwa tthu, a fascinating 'embassy' of the San people. There's a lovely restaurant, peaceful lawns upon which to relax and an excellently curated museum about the history of San peoples of the area.

- Further up the coast is the West Coast National Park, an absolute must-visit in spring. The wild flowers and coastal fynbos species are mind-blowingly beautiful. A tidal pool swim and visit to the park must surely be one of the loveliest ways to spend a day outside of Cape Town.

Silwerstroom Tidal Pool, Silwerstroom Resort, R27, Silwerstroomstrand

Size	51 m x 32 m
Swimmability	8
Facilities	Braai and picnic facilities, conference room, campsite, chalets and ablution facilities
Distance from Cape Town CBD	53 km
GPS coordinates	33°35'29.55"S 18°21'38.56"E
Disability access	Wheelchair accessible
General access	Silwerstroom Resort, small day-visitor fee
Safety	Safe swimming

ATLANTIC SEABOARD

Starting at the V&A Waterfront and ending in Hout Bay, the Atlantic Seaboard is a densely populated narrow cluster of suburbs and natural beaches that offers some of the most breathtaking views in the country. It is dotted with a vast array of restaurants, bars and cafés, and is sometimes called the Riviera of Cape Town. It contains some of the loveliest tidal pools of the Cape Peninsula, with fascinating history, all within an easy drive of each other.

The Atlantic Seaboard is known to be an exclusive area, but with a little effort, it can be a playground without being hugely expensive. The MyCiTi bus system offers a hop-on-hop-off way to travel, and Red Bus tours are available to deepen your knowledge of the area.

The tidal pools along this stretch of coast offer beauty, joy and respite from intense urban living, and are inclusive spaces in which to enjoy the Cape's well-known natural splendour. If you don't have a lot of time to drive out of town or go as far as Cape Point, visit one of these pools for mental and physical health reasons or simply to connect with other swimmers.

2 Graaff's Pool

Graaff's Pool was once the jewel of the area, with a long history of being well loved and frequented. It was built in 1907 by local businessman Pieter Marais; legend has it that he built it with a tunnel from his manor house (Villa Bordeaux) to shield his disabled wife from prying eyes on her way to the pool and as she bathed. The pool was named after its next owner, Sir Jacobus Arnoldus Combrinck Graaff, who donated it to the city in 1930. Prior to that it had been known as Below Bordeaux.

In the 1970s and 80s the pool was a popular spot for gay men, and became known as a gay nudist hangout, which scandalised some residents. An anecdote reflects the extent to which the goings-on at the pool caused a ruckus: a woman complained to authorities that she could see naked men at the pool from her home. A city official couldn't see anything from the window, to which she replied 'You can't see anything now, but when you stand on top of my dining room table with this pair of binoculars ...'

In 2005 the pool was damaged in a big storm, and instead of being repaired, it was demolished, one imagines partly in response to concerns about alleged activities occurring behind the wall.

Today, Graaff's Pool and its colourful history certainly justify a visit: the glamour of the past can still be imagined among slabs of concrete next to a beautiful natural cove. If you're very careful, you can make your way across the rocks, down some derelict steps and into a perfectly protected natural pool, 2–3 m deep and 15 m long, with a huge array of starfish, urchins and nudibranchs. This is next to the man-made pool – it is all that remains for a swimming area. It's unswimmable at high tide and in big swells, but at mid-tide it's one of the best-kept secrets on the Atlantic, especially if you want to avoid crowds. I love doing lengths here at sunrise in summer if the tide aligns – watching the light over Lion's Head while you're immersed in this astoundingly beautiful cold water cannot be beaten as a start to the day.

Milton Pool and Graaff's Pool are the only two pools that are nestled between lengths of Malmesbury shale. This soft black rock contributes to the arresting beauty of the pools.

Things to do nearby:

- You're spoilt for choice with things to do in the area: walk along the Sea Point Promenade and stop for ice cream along the way or hire a scooter or bicycle to make it a little more exciting. Stop at the train park or Putt-Putt area on the way to the lighthouse or pop into one of many local cafés and restaurants.
- Join a Segway tour to learn more about local history.
- Sea Point has several geocaches hidden in the area, which is a fun way to explore while searching for hidden containers.

A view of the original site of Graaff's Pool after demolition

- Visit Sea Point Swimming Pool on the promenade and a short walk from Graaff's Pool. It's a fantastic spot to take a refreshing dip while enjoying ocean views.
- Pop in to the sensitively landscaped Green Point Park, which has free outdoor gym facilities, a delightful café with delicious ice cream, well-kept lawns for picnicking and a play area for little children. The Labyrinth in the park is a lovely little maze to explore.

Graaff's Pool, Beach Road, Sea Point

Size	20 m x 5 m
Swimmability	1
Facilities	Nearby, along the promenade
Distance from Cape Town CBD	5 km
GPS coordinates	33°54'44.4"S 18°23'13.72"E
Disability access	Not disability friendly. There are steps to the beach and some broken concrete slabs to navigate in getting to the pool.
Safety	Safe swimming at low tide and in calm seas. Always visit in a group.

Milton Tidal Pool

3 Milton Tidal Pool

Built in 1910, Milton pool is situated in the heart of Milton Beach, Sea Point. It's a relatively small pool but is perfect for small children to splash in the shallow waters of the gently sloping sandy beach. It's a great spot to watch the sunset, and the shells that wash up on the shore can fascinate young and old with their beauty.

There is parking on Beach Road. Walk along the promenade, down some steps and across a small beach to reach it. Though it is plain by comparison with its more glamorous counterparts, such as Camps Bay and Miller's Point Tidal Pools, Milton pool is a dependable experience without much variability.

Relax on the beach while the children play in the shallows, safe in the knowledge that no unexpected waves are going to sweep them away. The beach is often strewn with kelp, so keep that in mind if you want a beach without decomposing kelp, which can be smelly. It goes without saying that in the high season it is extremely busy.

Milton pool is surrounded by natural Malmesbury shale formations, which can be seen only along this short section of coastline. This is what intrigued Darwin on his visit to the Cape. You can stand at the place where the shale meets the granite a little further south and look up to Lion's Head, which shows the sandstone layers. You are witnessing three distinct stages of geological evolution from one spot.

Things to do nearby:

- Take a stroll to the derelict Graaff's Pool (walk towards the lighthouse along the beach).
- Make use of the free outdoor gym equipment along the promenade.
- Check out the sculptures and other art installations along the promenade and take in the view from any number of benches scattered along the walkway.
- Explore the coastline from a different perspective by renting a kayak or joining a guided sea kayaking tour.

Milton Tidal Pool, off Beach Road, Sea Point

Size	20 m x 20 m
Swimmability	2
Facilities	Toilets, food vendors, parking area
Distance from Cape Town CBD	5 km
GPS coordinates	33°54'52.25"S 18°23'10.55"E
Disability access	Although the promenade is wheelchair friendly, the beach is not, as the tidal pool is accessed by steps from the promenade.
General access	Free entry
Safety	Safe swimming

The bathing pool at Sea Point (data unknown)

Saunders Rock Tidal Pool

4 Saunders Rock Tidal Pool

Nestled between massive granite boulders on Saunders Beach, Saunders Rock has to be one of the best places to watch the sunset. Saunders Rock Tidal Pool is the last pool before you round the point towards Camps Bay. Get there early enough to pick the best rock for your sunset picnic after a dip in the pool. When the southeaster is howling on the other side of the peninsula, sheltered Bantry Bay is often the best place to enjoy the outdoors.

There is ample parking in the street and a set of steps leads down to the beach and pool. The relaxed atmosphere lends itself to lazy summer picnics or early-morning dips. The large boulder to the right, if you're facing the pool, can be accessed via a few steps along a supporting wall, then a scramble to the top. At high tide, if you're brave, you can jump into the waters below and swim safely to the beach.

The pool itself is accessed via a little concrete walkway, which can be slippery at some times of the year, so take care. Steps lead into the pool but there's no hand railing and the bottom is covered in shells, so booties are advised. If it's not too busy and the visibility is good, Saunders Rock is a peaceful pool for snorkelling – an introduction to the colourful marine life of the pool. The water can be icy, so brace yourself! Basking on the rocks in the sun after a cold immersion is a delectable, and worthy, way to spend an afternoon.

Saunders Rock pool feels like Cinderella decked out for the ball. She glimmers, she entices, she invites and, ultimately, she dances the night away with you, leaving you with the sense of having been transformed by the experience. It'll leave you wanting more.

Things to do nearby:

- A walk down the Sea Point Promenade will take you past the historic Winchester Hotel, a great place to enjoy a drink on the balcony at sunset and take in the sights of the passing crowds.
- Sea Point Main Road is a hop, skip and a jump away from the pool. It's worth stopping at Kleinsky's Delicatessen for the best filled bagel known to mankind before or after your dip. Their coffee is absolutely divine too.

Saunders Rock Tidal Pool, Sea Point Promenade, Beach Road, Sea Point

Size	15 m x 9 m
Swimmability	1
Facilities	Full ablution facilities are sometimes open.
Distance from Cape Town CBD	6 km
GPS coordinates	33°55'27.8"S 18°22'37.35"E
Disability access	No wheelchair access
General access	Free entry
Safety	Safe swimming

MAIDEN'S COVE TIDAL POOLS

One of the main attractions of Maiden's Cove is its breathtaking views of the Atlantic Ocean, the Twelve Apostles and the iconic Table Mountain. The natural beauty of this location means it is a popular spot for both locals and tourists. But its history makes it one of the Cape's most beloved beaches.

During apartheid, it was one of the few stretches of beach that people of colour were allowed to access without threat of violence. As Albie Sachs, South African lawyer, activist, writer and former Constitutional Court judge, so elegantly observed:

> Heritage protection involves much more than simply looking after historic buildings, ancient battlegrounds and threatened fynbos. In our country, there are many natural physical features that have intense heritage significance. These include rivers, rocks, caves, pools, trees and even mountains. Community usage over long periods of time has invested these features with great historic, sometimes even spiritual, meaning.
>
> The use of Maiden's Cove is one such example. It has become more than just a public scenic reserve that has had formal legal protected status for seven decades. In the long years when apartheid reserved the white sands of Clifton and Camps Bay for white people only, persons classified as Non-European were told they could go to the less hospitable boulders and rocky pools of Maiden's Cove. And this was how over the years generations made this wild and unmanicured location a distinctive and specially loved place of their own.
>
> Families from the Bo-Kaap walked over the Nek down the Glen to the one spot where they could have undisturbed access to the sea. Families from the Cape Flats came in taxis and bakkies with whatever picnic fare they could muster. During the height of the resistance to apartheid, when schools would be closed, a valedictory end-of-year ceremony would be held at Maiden's Cove.

With this in mind, I encourage you to access Maiden's Cove with some reverence and recognition of its past – and enjoy it for the jewel it is and was.

Maiden's Cove is not just one beach but rather a collection of small coves and rocky outcrops. There are several small sandy areas and rocky pools where visitors can relax and sunbathe. While the water is often quite cold owing to the Atlantic Ocean currents, the two tidal pools at the same location offer refreshing swims in deep but safe waters. Both pools lie between Clifton 4th Beach and Glen Beach. The southern one, Maiden's Cove 1, is smaller and requires a higher tide, while Maiden's Cove 2 is swimmable 'off' tide. Celebrated for their captivating panoramas, these pools offer a serene juxtaposition of mountain grandeur and ocean majesty.

Maiden's Cove has picnic facilities with tables, benches and braai areas making it a popular spot for families and friends to gather for a truly South African experience. It is generally easily accessible, with parking areas nearby. However, it can get quite crowded, especially on weekends and during peak holiday seasons.

It is close to other popular attractions, such as Clifton's beaches, Camps Bay and the Table Mountain Cableway, making it convenient to combine a visit to Maiden's Cove with other activities in the area.

Note: Maiden's Cove is fenced, entrance is monitored and the gate opens at 8 a.m. in summer. The queues can be extremely long even at that time of the morning.

5 Maiden's Cove 1

Maiden's Cove 1, unceremoniously and unimaginatively named, is the first and smaller of the two pools as you wind your way down from Victoria Road towards the boulders and lawns that surround the pools. The turn left from Camps Bay is signposted, but the road is busy, so keep an eye out for it.

This one could be thought of as the slightly forgotten and less impressive of the two Maiden's Cove pools. Entered from a shelly beach, it is a simple no-frills, no-nonsense kind of pool. Children will enjoy the shallows and those who prefer waist-deep water will enjoy a dip towards the deeper end of the pool. The pleasure really comes from the spectacular views when you're in the pool – of the Atlantic and her tumultuous waves, dramatic clouds over the Twelve Apostles and sprawling Camps Bay Beach beyond the granite boulders that surround the pools.

The pool is often empty if the tide hasn't been high enough to flush it.

Maiden's Cove 1, off Victoria Road, Camps Bay

Size	18 m x 26 m
Swimmability	1
Facilities	Full ablution facilities, braai and picnic areas open 8 a.m. to 6 p.m.
Distance from Cape Town CBD	7 km
GPS coordinates	33°56'42.74"S 18°22'28.93"E
Disability access	With difficulty
General access	Free entry
Safety	Safe swimming

Maiden's Cove 2

❻ Maiden's Cove 2

The more sophisticated of the two pools, if such a thing is possible, Maiden's Cove 2 offers depth and the opportunity to stretch out and do a few widths. There are some hidden rocks but when the visibility is good, this pool is a quiet gem. It is best entered by jumping off one of the side walls, but those who are less adventurous can go in from the beach, taking their time to adjust to the cold water. It is increasingly becoming a popular sunset spot, so get there early enough to get a place on one of the boulders, along the lawn or on the small shelly beach.

Things to do nearby:

- Take a stroll towards Camps Bay and follow the signs down to the protected Glen Beach, a relatively small beach nestled between huge boulders.
- A walk or drive to nearby Camps Bay opens up the possibility of numerous restaurants, bars and cafés to suit a range of preferences.

Maiden's Cove 2, off Victoria Road, Camps Bay

Size	36 m x 20 m
Swimmability	5
Facilities	Full ablution facilities. Braai and picnic areas open 8 a.m. to 6 p.m.
Distance from Cape Town CBD	7 km
GPS coordinates	33°56'41.57"S 18°22'24.49"E
Disability access	The walkway takes you within range of the pool but not into it.
General access	Free entry
Safety	Safe swimming

7 Camps Bay Tidal Pool

Camps Bay was, historically, considered too cold and dangerous to swim in. By 1901 palm trees had been planted in New Brighton, as it was then known, and within a few years kerbed roads were being built. Accessibility was a challenge, but by 1910 motorbuses were running. Camps Bay got its first public swimming pool in 1904, which formed part of a pavilion. Later, in 1913, a municipal amalgamation saw the City Council instruct local developers Cape Marine Suburbs (a company owned by two randlords, who also owned most of the property in Camps Bay and who, rather conveniently, seemed to be awarded most of the development tenders for the area), together with a local engineer and local Parks and Recreation committee, to invest in the development and improvement of the area. One of the 'improvements' was the construction of a seawall at Lime Kiln Bay, which created a substantial pool – the current site of Camps Bay Tidal Pool. A pavilion was built near the pool, which included bathing cabins and tearooms. It also included a place for concerts, with the audience expected to sit on the sand.

In 1918 Camps Bay was described thus in *Cape Peninsula Holiday Haunts*:

> Camp's Bay [*sic*] itself is a restorative health resort, ozone from driven salt spray, balm from adjacent pine woods, and cool, fresh mountain airs mingle on the Camp's Bay beach and constitute just the tonic needed to send new life to tissues parched by inland heat.
>
> The Camp's Bay beach is pleasant and uncommon. Unlike so many seafronts, it is not a depressing range of furze-clad sand dunes, but a restful, charming pleasure-ground where grassy downs and long silvery strands alternate with picturesque rocky coves and promontories.
>
> The beach slopes too abruptly, and the currents are too strong to permit surf bathing, but there are places specially indicated by signboards, where open sea bathing may be enjoyed in water calm, safe and deep enough in places to permit of swimming, and shallow enough in other places to accommodate those who do not swim.

Today, Camps Bay Tidal Pool is popular with families, visitors and serious outdoor swimmers training for open-water swims. The pool is just off Victoria Road, with a MyCiTi bus stop right opposite, making it easily accessible from the city centre. There is parking along the main road and up side roads near the pool, and car guards provide a modicum of security that your car will remain where it was left while you enjoy a few hours in the sublime icy waters of the pool.

There are two small beaches separated by an ablution block. You can also walk along the walls of the pool and enter at the steps provided or jump in or walk in from one of the two beaches.

The pool, at sunrise, welcomes people ranging from middle-aged dippers to tough distance swimmers. Later in the day, the families arrive and, towards sunset, the picnickers enjoy one of the best views of the pool and ocean beyond, Lion's Head to the right and the

Twelve Apostles to the left. The pool is often sheltered from the southeaster; however, when the wind picks up and the tablecloth comes over the mountain behind you, you have about 20 minutes before the wind reaches the pool and the surface becomes choppy.

Camps Bay Tidal Pool is generally underrated. On a quieter day it houses starfish (check the corners of the pool), an elusive octopus (often seen gliding between the rocks close to the beach on the left), a variety of seaweeds and tiny snails moving along the walls.

A popular activity is swimming to the back wall as fast as you can and then clambering up to wait for the waves to knock you off when the tide is high. It's also a fantastic pool in which children can learn to swim or adults can improve their fitness by swimming in quadrangles around the pool or along the back wall.

Camps Bay is where it all started for me, and remains a firm favourite when I wander to that side of the world. Camps Bay pool never feels tempestuous – she's a calm old friend with a playful nature, ready to entice even the most reticent of dippers to become a more robust swimmer. If you allow her to, she'll help you see things in a different light, and leave you calm and at peace.

Things to do nearby:

- Visit Theatre on the Bay for the latest production.
- Grab a pizza from a local restaurant and enjoy a sunset picnic on the beach.
- Frolic in the waves at Camps Bay Beach a few hundred metres away.
- Enjoy the astounding views of the area.

Camps Bay Tidal Pool, Victoria Road, Camps Bay

Size	61 m x 42 m
Swimmability	10
Facilities	Ablutions at the pool
Distance from Cape Town CBD	7 km
GPS coordinates	33°57'17.8"S 18°22'32.05"E
Disability access	Accessible via a ramp
General access	Free entry
Safety	Safe swimming for adults and kids

Lime Kiln Bay before and after enclosure to create a tidal pool. (Postcard D. Watts and the NLSA)

The paddling pool at Camps Bay (opened 1910)

KOMMETJIE/SLANGKOP

Kommetjie can feel like a sleepy fishing village by the sea when you're in Kommetjie proper, despite being a divided society, with Ocean View and Masiphumelele on its borders and relationships between the three often strained.

A walk along Kommetjie's long white sandy beaches, around the point, marked by a huge log, takes you to Long Beach. Gazing across the bay from Kommetjie offers a truly astounding view of Noordhoek Peak, Hout Bay's Sentinel and an ocean that can be deep blue or aquamarine in colour. The sea in Kommetjie is deeply alluring but you'll need a wetsuit – or a lot of courage – to brave the ocean here, because it is always notably cold. The beach is great for horse-riding, dog-walking and windsurfing and boasts some of the best waves to surf on the South Peninsula.

The famous Slangkop Lighthouse derives its name from the Slangkop (Snakehead) hill behind it. It has been burning brightly since 1914 (although it is far from the first lighthouse to function in South Africa: that was The Green Point Lighthouse, which was first lit in 1824). It's possible to tour the lighthouse by arrangement.

Kommetjie is known for its old milkwood groves, which line some of the beaches and parks and are protected by law.

Die Kom Tidal Pool

8 Die Kom Tidal Pool

A scenic drive to consider taking is Chapman's Peak Drive linking Hout Bay to Noordhoek. Use this route if travelling from Camps Bay Tidal Pool to Die Kom in Kommetjie and you won't be sorry.

Die Kom is situated on the corner of Beach Road and Van Imhoff Way in Kommetjie, the tiny but up-and-coming village along the Atlantic, past Noordhoek. The name of the village means 'small basin', in Afrikaans. Kommetjie is located around a small natural cove that resembles a basin. It's believed that early inhabitants used this basin as a fish trap. The wall that enclosed this tidal pool was demolished a few decades ago, leaving the basin behind. A few metres of the wall that once enclosed the pool can still be seen at low tide. The natural basin is still good for swimming but only at high tide, when it gets deep enough, and when the water quality improves with fresher seawater flowing in. In fact, water quality is the biggest challenge for this pool, and the City of Cape Town rated it as 'poor' in October 2023. Be aware of this, but it is generally considered safe to swim.

The easiest entrance to the original pool is via a small beach next to the boat launch parking, though this part of the bay is no longer the preferred swimming spot. The popular alternative is to access the natural basin of the actual Kom via two old crayfish boat launches located off the catwalk that snakes from a lovely grassy area along the fringe of the milkwoods all the way to the iconic Slangkop Lighthouse. You'll need to make your way down the concrete slipways, over rocks that are sometimes slippery, and then push off the rocks in an inelegant belly flop to get into the water. Locals gather on the rocks next to the boat launches when the tide is high for an evening dip in summer and winter alike. It's also a wonderful secret swim spot when the southeaster is ravaging the rest of Cape Town – it is somewhat sheltered even from strong gusts and the water is usually a few degrees warmer than the cold Atlantic Ocean, since the pool is quite shallow. The size of the pool lends itself to laps and training swims except when there's swell ... or, if you're a strong swimmer looking for a protected challenge, especially if there is swell.

On calm evenings when the wind isn't howling, you'll might see puffadder shysharks lurking in the pool.

There are many places to park, but it is easiest to park in the lot next to Die Kom, walk past the grassy picnic area, and then make your way to the slipways to the water. It isn't advisable to enter the water from the grassy embankment where steps descend into the pool, as it is very shallow and rocky here and the kelp accumulates, making it tricky to get into the water; added to which, there is a well-known resident Cape cobra that keeps the area free of rats.

Things to do nearby:

- Stop at the Imhoff Farm Deli for supplies and enjoy a sunset picnic on the grassy lawn overlooking the cove.
- Stroll along the boardwalk to Kommetjie Lighthouse, an incredibly scenic walk. Bring some tea or coffee to enjoy on one of the many benches along the way.
- Take a walk along the beach in Kommetjie, round the corner below a large washed-up log, and head to Long Beach, Noordhoek. Not too far from Kommetjie, you will find the washed-up shipwreck of SS *Kakapo*, which ran aground in 1900; owing to the movement of the sand, various parts of it are visible at different times.

Die Kom, Kommetjie (1925)

- If you have time, tackle the 5.5-km walk along the beach to Noordhoek parking lot. A few kilometres down the road, you can enjoy a cold drink and an authentic Italian pizza at Limoncello.
- At low tide, rock-pooling near the beach in Kommetjie produces hidden gems of sea life.
- In spring, the walkway along Die Kom is dotted with beautiful fynbos flowers.

Die Kom Tidal Pool, Lighthouse Road, Kommetjie

Size	Original pool: 30 m x 100 m Die Kom (natural basin): 100 m x 200 m
Swimmability	6 at high tide
Facilities	Picnic facilities
Distance from Cape Town CBD	44 km
GPS coordinates	34°08'34.63"S 18°19'19.71"E
Disability access	No wheelchair access
General access	No entry fee
Safety	Safe swimming in Die Kom basin when the conditions are right.

SOETWATER TIDAL POOLS

Just a hop and a skip past the Slangkop Lighthouse lies a conservancy with not one but two enchanting pools. These aren't your run-of-the-mill pools: their location is perfect. Plonk your towel down near either pool and, like magic, your central nervous system goes into full relaxation mode. The natural beauty is like something out of a fairy tale, and there's a gentle vibe that wraps around the pools like a cosy blanket.

The two pools in Soetwater Resort are not accessible from Kommetjie village itself, even though they are near (and Google might say otherwise): there is a locked gate across Lighthouse Road. Instead, you must drive 4 km south along the beautifully scenic hillside pass out of Kommetjie (M65) to a turnoff marked Soetwater; drive another kilometre to the gate, where an entrance fee is payable, and a further 3 km to the pools. It is 8 km from Die Kom to the Soetwater Tidal Pools via the road.

Soetwater 1

9 Soetwater 1

The larger of the two pools, Soetwater 1 is the first on the left if you are driving towards the Slangkop Lighthouse on Lighthouse Road.

Soetwater is one of the last vestiges of pristine coastal terrace on the Cape Peninsula – an intricate tapestry of rocky shores, flourishing dune ecosystems, seasonal wetlands, coastal plains and mountain scree slopes. Adding to its historical richness are three ancient Khoisan fish traps (*visvywers*), carefully preserved along the Soetwater coastline.

Nestled between the sea and the ancient Slangkop hillside, this slender coastal stretch boasts an incredible diversity of life. It's a haven for endangered oystercatchers, and has otter and caracal families. Just beyond the waves, you'll find dense kelp beds, while along the shoreline, a series of distinctive coastal wetland lagoons adds to its charm.

Folks from the neighbouring Ocean View, and further afield Athlone, Elsies River, Bothasig and Bonteheuwel, have been frequenting this place for generations, making Soetwater a destination with deeper relevance to the broader Cape Town community.

The tidal pool is accessed via a security gate at which you pay a nominal entrance fee per person. Overlooking the pool are grassy terraces close to clean ablution facilities with freshwater showers. A few hundred metres from the pool, braai facilities nestle under shaded pergolas. The area is safe for children to explore along the sandy shore or on the lawns. The children's pool doesn't easily fill or empty of water, so it's important to check the water quality before swimming – if it looks murky or like a welcoming place for flies, stay clear. The main pool, which is relatively shallow, is enclosed by a half-moon-shaped wall over which waves crash at high tides, bringing with them kelp fronds. In the quieter off-season this is a lovely day trip for swimming lengths and enjoying the pristine wilderness.

Things to do nearby:

- Take bicycles with you and enjoy a ride along flat, safe roads towards the lighthouse and back to the pool for a picnic and a dip.
- The campsite at Soetwater, which has electricity at some sites and clean ablution facilities, is situated beyond a security gate with guard.
- Leave the conservancy for a walk along Witsand Beach, which has to be one of the best-kept secrets in Cape Town at spring time, when the fynbos and wildflowers create a colourful landscape along the dunes and narrow path towards Misty Cliffs.
- Witsand offers some excellent waves for beginner surfers.
- When the wind is up, Witsand is packed with wind-sport fans, which makes for fascinating viewing as the kites fly like colourful but slightly demented bats.

Soetwater 1, Lighthouse Road, Soetwater Resort

Size	35 m x 38 m
Swimmability	5
Facilities	Braai area, picnic sites and toilets, which all visitors can use.
Distance from Cape Town CBD	45 km
GPS coordinates	34°09'30.12"S 18°19'38.18"E
Disability access	Sort of, via a crumbly concrete ramp
General access	Entrance fee payable at the gate of the resort. The conservancy isn't always open, so check opening and closing times.
Safety	Family safe

10 Soetwater 2

To reach Soetwater 2, drive into the campsite via a guarded boom. Slightly smaller than its counterpart, this pool feels cosy, which is unusual for a body of water. Its temperature is higher than that of the larger pool, because it is shallower. Despite this, the back wall allows waves to wash over, keeping the water a bit fresher, especially during high tide.

During spring tide, the water level significantly drops, and it may become murky. It's advisable to check the tides before your visit to ensure you go when the pool is brimming with fresh saltwater. Ample parking is available off-season, but during peak season the campsite attracts a multitude of holidaymakers.

Things to do nearby:

- Keep an eye out for the speedy white-fronted sandplover and the black oystercatcher – they're the ones laying their eggs in the seaweed on the beaches. And if you're lucky you might spot dune mole rats, tortoises and grysbok on the dunes.
- In the off-seasons (autumn and spring) camping can be one of the most wonderful ways to spend a night. The stars are incredible if the skies are clear, which makes this one of the best stargazing sites close to the city. There are a number of excellent stargazing books available (see the back of this book for a recommendation), so be sure to take one with you, and a telescope for best viewing.
- Book a coastal foraging adventure and meal at Veld & Sea, run by Cape Town locals Roushanna and Tom Gray, who are based near Cape Point.

Soetwater 2, Lighthouse Road, Soetwater Resort

Size	35 m x 30 m
Swimmability	5
Facilities	Braai pits, picnic tables and toilets available
Distance from Cape Town CBD	46 km
GPS coordinates	34°09'14.95"S 18°19'20.55"E
Disability access	Partial, but not well maintained
General access	Entrance fee payable at the gate of the resort. The conservancy isn't always open, so check opening and closing times.
Safety	Safe swimming and the resort in general is safe.

CAPE POINT NATURE RESERVE

Situated at the southern tip of the Cape Peninsula, approximately 60 km south of Cape Town, Cape Point is part of the southern section of Table Mountain National Park. The park spans 7 750 ha and is renowned for its diverse fauna and flora. It forms part of the Cape Floral Kingdom, which is a World Heritage Site.

Within the park, one finds a dynamic landscape that serves as a playground for both visitors and native wildlife, including baboons and other wild animals. The area has an array of incredible hikes and overnight accommodation options, and is steeped in the rich history of the Cape.

Cape Point has beautiful beaches, two tidal pools and an excellent natural rock pool, strategically positioned to offer spectacular views. For those spending the day in the reserve, these pools can form a three-part tidal pool hop. It's advisable to arrive early, particularly during the peak of summer, to avoid the long queues at the entrance.

The wildlife at Cape Point is abundant. The lawns surrounding the tidal pools were previously used as campsites or cultivated land. These open spaces have allowed non-indigenous grasses to take root, which attracts larger antelope that are not able to survive on the nutrient-poor fynbos. This makes these open areas good places to find bontebok and eland grazing. However, baboons are also fond of these areas and can be dangerous; do not feed them and try to keep a safe distance. It's best to keep any excess food in your car when you're picnicking. Sharks too can be a danger in the open ocean at Cape Point – don't swim too far out!

Buffels Bay Tidal Pool

11 Buffels Bay Tidal Pool

To get to the Buffels Bay pool drive 7.8 km from the pay gate towards Cape Point, passing the turnoff to Bordjiesrif and the Buffelsfontein visitor centre, both on your left. Just a short distance on, look for the next left turn marked Buffels Bay. Take this turn and drive to the sea 850 m away. The pool is on the left of this road next to a slipway.

Equipped with braai facilities and surrounded by old milkwood groves, Buffels Bay pool offers the most comfortable experience of the three pools in the reserve. Ample parking is available, and a brief stroll down a gentle slope leads to the pool.

The pool, the deepest in the reserve, has multiple entry points, with stone steps leading to a shallow rocky area or the option to walk along the walls and jump in. The back wall marks the deepest point of the pool: chest depth. In periods of light or no winds, the marine life within the pool is a spectacular sight.

Buffels Bay pool offers a great environment for those learning to snorkel, engaging in leisurely laps or simply enjoying the water. Children spend hours splashing around, honing their diving skills and exploring the nooks and crannies between the pools.

It's important to acknowledge the historical context as well: during the apartheid era, this pool was designated for 'white use only' while the nearby pool at Bordjiesrif was designated for 'coloured use only'.

Things to do nearby:

- Explore the beach adjacent to the pool or jump in for a surf at a spot called Black Rocks (unimaginatively named but helpful in identifying where a good reef break can be found, though the waves are unreliable). Winter is the best time to surf here.
- Explore the milkwood grove within a 100-m walk of the pool. Settle under the trees and take some deep breaths – the rich earthy fragrance is intoxicating, and the sense of how old these trees are is palpable.
- The Gifkommetjie to Hoek van Bobbejaan walk is on the Atlantic side of the promontory (a short drive from Buffels Bay). The walk is a four-hour round trip, which starts along the spiny ridge leading down to the beach; the wreck of the trawler *Phyllisia* can be explored, before you make your way along the coast and through a narrow milkwood tunnel back to the main path, which ascends to the parking lot. Explore the beach along this stretch of coast for flotsam and jetsam after a storm.
- Take the Flying Dutchman funicular at Cape Point up to the old lighthouse and enjoy spectacular views.

Buffels Bay Tidal Pool, Cape Point Nature Reserve

Size	50 m x 24 m
Swimmability	6
Facilities	Picnic areas, braai spots and toilets Cape Point offers shops, restaurants, picnics, hikes and cultural and historical spots all within a few kilometres of the pool.
Distance from Cape Town CBD	60 km
GPS coordinates	34°19'14.51"S 18°27'40.72"E
Disability access	Not disability friendly
General access	In order to qualify for SA rates, you must present a valid SA ID or passport (the SANParks My Green Card gives SA citizens 12 free entries to any Table Mountain NP pay point).
Safety	Safe swimming

Bordjiesrif Tidal Pool

12 Bordjiesrif Tidal Pool

After you have entered the reserve, drive for 6.6 km towards Cape Point and look out for the first turnoff to the left, marked with a low sign saying Bordjiesrif. Follow this road for 2 km to the sea, where you will find a car park next to the pool.

During apartheid, Bordjiesrif was reserved for 'coloured use only'. Today, it is a well-loved pool that offers shallow, sandy-bottomed swimming and easy entrance via a broad stretch off the wall closest to the lawn. The pool is overlooked by terraced lawns but the baboons also favour it, owing to the easy-pickings from the picnickers.

In the reserve, two symbolic *padrões* (stone monuments) commemorate the voyages of discovery of Portuguese explorers Bartolomeu Dias and Vasco da Gama. Beyond their commemorative role, these structures serve as vital navigational warnings for sailors. The Dias Padrão, painted black on one side for enhanced visibility against the skyline, graces a hill near Buffelsfontein Peak. The Da Gama Padrão is near Bordjiesrif. When sighted from False Bay, these *padrões* align to indicate the direction of the submerged Whittle Rock – a shipping hazard that is now additionally marked by a buoy. In 1988, a smaller *padrão* was erected at Buffels Bay to mark the quincentenary of Dias's historic landing at the Cape.

Things to do nearby:

- Find shade under the bank of old milkwoods along the length of the picnic area.
- Look out for grazing antelope and elusive zebras.

Bordjiesrif Tidal Pool, Cape Point Nature Reserve

Size	50 m x 24 m
Swimmability	4
Facilities	Toilets, picnic area Cape Point offers shops, restaurants, picnics, hikes and cultural and historical spots all within a few kilometres of the pool.
Distance from Cape Town CBD	60 km
GPS coordinates	34°18'48.07"S 18°27'42.98"E
Disability access	No wheelchair access
General access	In order to qualify for SA rates, you must present a valid SA ID or passport (the SANParks My Green Card gives SA citizens 12 free entries to any Table Mountain NP pay point).
Safety	Safe swimming

13 Venus Pool

Start your journey to the enchanting Venus Pool from Cape Point's entrance gate. Follow the tarred road from the park's entrance, turn left at the Bordjiesrif turnoff, then take another left, bypassing the sign for Bordjiesrif. Continue until the road ends, and you'll find parking options to the right or in front of the old kiln.

From the parking area you'll need to walk 1 km to the end of the road, which narrows to a footpath. There is a sign to the right that identifies Venus Pool. Climb down a series of flat rocks to reach the pool, and access its embrace from the rocky sides. During high tide, waves crash dramatically over the protective rocks, adding a touch of excitement with a deep, resonant boom.

Venus Pool is a haven for swimming, surrounded by a vibrant array of sea life, including fish, giant starfish, urchins in various hues, crabs, clean green seaweed, anemones, black mussels and barnacles. The flat rocks are perfect spots to relax like basking seals next to this gorgeous little pool.

Take sunscreen and umbrellas with you, as there's no shade at the pool. It is advisable to wear sea shoes: there are colourful urchins awaiting uncovered feet.

If you're exploring nearby attractions at Cape Point, consider letting go of the need to do more, and simply 'be' at Venus Pool. Breathe, immerse yourself in the beauty, and let the surroundings captivate you.

Venus Pool, Cape Point Nature Reserve

Size	20 m x 6 m
Swimmability	3
Facilities	No ablutions. Cape Point offers shops, restaurants, picnics, hikes and cultural and historical spots all within a few kilometres of the pool.
Distance from Cape Town CBD	61 km (one on foot)
GPS coordinates	34°17'48.84"S 18°28'01.02"E
Disability access	No wheelchair access
General access	In order to qualify for SA rates, you must present a valid SA ID or passport (the SANParks My Green Card gives SA citizen 12 free entries to any Table Mountain NP pay point).
Safety	Safe for snorkelling. The rocks are slippery when wet.

FALSE BAY

False Bay is considered one of the great bays of the Western Cape and sweeps from Cape Point to Hangklip. Between these two points are numerous neighbourhoods, stretches of coast, pristine fynbos, the odd troop of baboons, a penguin colony, visiting southern right whale pods, cliffs, tidal pools, surfing beaches and more.

The tidal pools along the False Bay coastline are considered jewels in the crown of the Cape Peninsula. The St James, Dalebrook, Kalk Bay and Woolley's pools were all completed between 1911 and 1914. All the tidal pools of False Bay were initially built illegally before various official government bodies took over their management. It is the story of all these pools that someone, in the course of history, took it upon themselves to illegally build a wall or an enclosed area where they felt it necessary. When the cost of maintenance became too arduous, the builder inevitably approached the necessary governing body to either take it over or pay for the maintenance. None of the pools built in this way were retained by private individuals, but it is interesting to note the extent to which today's locals take proud responsibility for supporting the city in maintenance or improvements.

Miller's Point Tidal Pool

14 Miller's Point Tidal Pool

Miller's Point is the hidden gem among the False Bay tidal pools, tucked away as it is behind a man-made dune. Named after Edmund Miller, who began operating a whaling station there in 1825, the pool has shed its cruel history and is now a place for good old R & R. Positioned between two boat slipways, it uniquely boasts a slide, a feature absent from other tidal pools.

To reach Miller's Point, drive south from Simon's Town on Main Road. Pass Boulders Beach and continue for about 5 km, past the Miller's Point Recreation Area, until you reach the sign for the Miller's Point pool. This spot is also used by the boat club for launching: on weekends and during holidays the parking area is full of boat trailers. The pool can be reached either by a longer walk around the dune via the slipway road or by curving around the dune along the sandy footpath near the sea.

Around the pool, there are shaded spots and lawns frequented by dedicated holiday-makers during the high season. The pool itself is a favourite with kids.

There are two entry points into the pool via uneven steps with handrails. The surrounding walls also offer jumping access. A central rock provides a perch to bask on or seek refuge from choppy waves.

Large boulders to the left when you face the sea provide opportunities for scrambling when the waters are clear. Miller's Point is an ideal training pool, often less crowded during quieter off-season months. There are beautiful natural rock pools in the vicinity for a more adventurous dip.

However, because of its remote setting, crime may pose a concern, so it's advisable to visit in groups and leave valuables at home. A local troop of baboons is known to be extremely brazen, so take care with any food.

Things to do nearby:

- On your way there, stop at the Sweetest Thing French patisserie in Simon's Town for a coffee and pastry.
- Visit Boulders Penguin Colony.
- Meander along Main Road Simon's Town, popping into the quirky shops along the way.
- Stop at the nearby naval museum or cemetery for a sense of the long history of the town and the many men, women and children who contributed to it.
- Take a ghost tour of Simon's Town.

- This stretch of coast offers some of the best freediving in the world – it's worth making a plan to explore the kelp forests off the various slipways, but look out for kayakers and boats as these are popular spots to launch when there's a fish run.
- Beware of sharks, especially when there's a fish run just off the coast.
- On the way back, stop at the Lighthouse Cafe in Simon's Town; their lunches are next level!

Miller's Point Tidal Pool, Main Road, Simon's Town

Size	64 m x 37 m
Swimmability	10
Facilities	Ablutions, changing rooms, braai spots, grassy spots for a picnic
Distance from Cape Town CBD	47 km
GPS coordinates	34°13'52.53"S 18°28'33.55"E
Disability access	No wheelchair access
General access	Free entry
Safety	Go in a group; watch out for baboons.

15 Shelley Point Tidal Pool

Located along a dirt road approximately 300 m south of Glencairn Tidal Pool, the beautiful, derelict Shelley Point pool awaits discovery. To find it, park near the station and walk towards Simon's Town.

The pool affords some of the best whale-watching on the peninsula. Swim towards the main wall and position yourself with your back against it. The wall's foundation has a ledge made of rocks and pebbles. Before long, a wave will break over you – a bracing experience.

The pool backs onto a small sandy beach and in years gone by it was one of the most popular pools in the area. Now it is used more for dips than day-long stretches, but it's great for very young children who are gaining confidence in the water.

Things to do nearby:

- Climb Elsie's Peak, which overlooks Fish Hoek – an easy enough walk.
- Join a local swimming group early in the morning for laps along the beach at Glencairn, just beyond the breakers, when conditions are right.
- Dive the wreck of the *Clan Stuart* to the left of the beach at Dido Valley/Glen Marine, a short swim from the beach, for some remarkable underwater magic.
- Explore the old naval relics, such as the huge 9.2-inch gun at the Scala Battery on a hill-side overlooking the harbour.

Shelley Point Tidal Pool, Main Road, Glencairn

Size	17 m x 13 m
Swimmability	2
Facilities	Parking and toilets at Glencairn station
Distance from Cape Town CBD	37 km
GPS coordinates	34°10'05.27"S 18°25'53.95"E
Disability access	No wheelchair access
General access	By foot, no entrance fee
Safety	Safe swimming

16 Glencairn Tidal Pool

Glencairn Tidal Pool, positioned next to the Glencairn station, is one of the larger pools in the area, although not easily visible from the road. It was built in the 1920s, when it was hugely popular. It remains a favourite owing to its sandy bottom, offering a user-friendly experience and the assurance of avoiding accidental encounters with urchins. Access is either via a small sandy beach or by walking along the walls and taking a dive.

The pool's deepest section, closest to the back wall, is about chest-deep, while the rest is, at best, waist-deep. This feature makes it popular with children, who spend hours playing in the pool during summer and winter. To the right of the pool, near the beach, a few rocks create a safe natural barrier, allowing children to enjoy trawling with fishing nets as silvery shoals gracefully avoid capture.

Glencairn is an excellent pool for various activities, from learning to swim and building confidence in the water to whale watching. Its azure waters seamlessly blend with the vast ocean beyond. The sandy beach is adorned with shells and, at low tide, to the left of the pool, children can explore rock pools teeming with sea life.

A leisurely stroll along the cement walkway leads to Glencairn Beach, which is great for boogie-boarding and, on calm days, swimming lengths along the beach.

Conveniently located next to the station, Glencairn is one of the few pools easily accessible by train (when it is running). Please take care when crossing the railway line.

There is parking along the road or next to the station (station staff often keep an eye on nearby parked cars in exchange for tips). The pool is visited by a diverse community that comfortably shares the space.

Things to do nearby:

- To the left of the beach is a kelp forest with decent drop-off just beyond the kelp. This is an easy, accessible dive spot to visit close to the beach, with an astounding array of sea life.
- Just off the small beach at Dido Valley before you get to Simon's Town is the SS *Clan Stuart* wreck, which is partially visible above the water. Today, she is the site of marvellous diving only a short distance from the beach. Her sister ship, the *Clan Monroe*, was wrecked in 1905 just off the lighthouse at Kommetjie ... an unlucky family.

Glencairn Tidal Pool, Main Road, Glencairn

Size	50 m x 25 m
Swimmability	3
Facilities	No facilities, but there is a toilet at the station; pack a picnic and eat on the beach.
Distance from Cape Town CBD	36.5 km
GPS coordinates	34°09'45.97"S 18°25'56.08"E
Disability access	No wheelchair access
General access	Free entry
Safety	Safe swimming

17 Skellies Pool

Skellies (Skeleton) Pool, a natural tidal pool surrounded by rocks, has steps and a handrail for easier access. While the handrail may initially seem excessive given how tiny the pool is, it is invaluable when waves are rough.

To reach Skellies Pool, you can either walk along Jager's Walk from Fish Hoek Beach or park on Main Road, cross the railway line at Sunny Cove station pedestrian bridge, turn left at the bottom of the steps and walk about 120 m down the walkway until you discover the pool tucked between some boulders.

This lovely tucked-away pool is ideal for leisurely dips. Although some daring individuals may opt to dive into the ocean from the surrounding rocks and swim to the beach, this practice is not advisable due to the return of great white sharks to the bay. When the beach is busy, Skellies is often a protected spot for a dip with far fewer visitors.

Skellies is believed to be the original site of a fish trap, with embedded bolts in the rock hinting at its potential use for whaling decades ago.

Things to do nearby:

- Spend some time in the Bookworm in nearby Fish Hoek for a great range of quality second-hand books.
- Pop to Fish Hoek Beach for boogie-boarding within the safety of the shark nets, which are erected each morning and retracted in the evening in summer.
- Take a walk along Fish Hoek Beach to Clovelly corner and back. This is a safe walk and dogs are allowed.

Skellies Pool, Main Road, Fish Hoek

Size	7 m x 5 m
Swimmability	2
Facilities	None, but walk to Fish Hoek Beach to access ablutions
Distance from Cape Town CBD	35 km
GPS coordinates	34°08'35.14"S 18°26'07.3"E
Disability access	No wheelchair access
General access	Access via the beach along Jager's Walk or via the bridge over the railway line onto Jager's Walk
Safety	Great for a plunge, dangerous at high tide or in big swells

Woolley's Tidal Pool

18 Woolley's Tidal Pool

Named after William Woolley, the man who built it, this small pool offers astounding views and is well worth a visit for that alone. Legend has it that Mr Woolley, who completed the pool in 1914, either built it himself or stewarded the space and requested the municipality to enclose it with a cement wall, after which they took over its maintenance and management. Mr Woolley and his family resided in a house called Wayside; the pool, a short walk away, offered relief from the summer heat.

As you round the corner towards Fish Hoek from Kalk Bay, find parking as soon as possible: the pool is accessed via steps to the left of the walkway. Go down the steps and under the railway and you will find the little pool and its smaller children's pool in front of you.

Woolley's has flat rocks that are ideal for sunbathing. A deep shelf just to the right of the pool is accessed over the rocks at low tide and when it's flat you can dive in a pristine kelp forest. Woolley's is brimful of multicoloured urchins, shells, anemones and shoals of little silvery fish. Despite its charm it is isolated, and visiting in a group is advisable.

Things to do nearby:

- Visit nearby Kalk Bay, where you can choose from a host of restaurants with a tempting array of delicious snacks and meals. Olympia Bakery is renowned for its fresh pastries and breads but get there early to avoid missing out. If you grab a coffee and pastry first thing in the morning you can enjoy them on the rocks next to the pool as the sun rises.
- Kalk Bay is a historical fishing village with a single main road meandering between quirky shops, which are fun to explore. There are also plenty of interesting places down the side roads.

Woolley's Tidal Pool, off Main Road, Kalk Bay

Size	20 m x 11 m
Swimmability	3
Facilities	Picnic on the rocks
Distance from Cape Town CBD	32 km
GPS coordinates	34°07'57.94"S 18°26'43.79"E
Disability access	No wheelchair access
General access	Access via subway under the railway line
Safety	Safe swimming

Three girls at Woolley's Tidal Pool, 1908. Likely relatives of William Woolley

William Woolley, b. 1841, Pangbourne, Berkshire

KALK BAY TIDAL POOLS

Kalk Bay Tidal Pools 1 & 2 are adjacent to each other and can be accessed via the subway under the railway line near the Kalk Bay station entrance. Once you reach the top of the steps, the pools will be directly in front of you, partially obscured from view by the restaurant built up around the site. There are two benches next to the pool and a freshwater shower to the left of the pool. These two pools provide a generous space for swimming and are filled with abundant sea life.

One of the delights of these pools – and I may be taken to task for sharing this closely guarded secret – is that there's a hole in the wall between them. It is large enough to swim through and lined with urchins. Children love swimming through the hole over and over, and few repeat the mistake of touching the sides and getting pricked by an urchin.

19 Kalk Bay 1

Kalk Bay 1 is a natural cove in front of Kalk Bay station. It was initially known as Bishop's Pool, a name bestowed in honour of Bishop Robert Gray, the Anglican Bishop of Cape Town. During the 1860s and 1870s, Bishop Gray frequented this spot for bathing while on holiday in Kalk Bay. This locale was not only a popular informal bathing area but may also have served as a fish trap.

In 1911 Charles McGhie was commissioned by the Kalk Bay municipality to formalise Bishop's Pool. As part of this effort, a lengthy pool was created, allowing entry via a gently sloping sandy beach that extended from the railway embankment. In 1913, a protective wall was constructed at one end of the pool to prevent the accumulation of sand and silt within the pool. Once open to men only, it is now – and has been for a long time – open to everyone.

To enter the pool, some folks go in via the steps to the left. These are usually overgrown with seaweed and can be very slippery – even with the handrail, it makes for a tricky and at times undignified entrance. It is best to walk down the steps on the sea side, take a little step over the gap in the wall that allows the pool to drain, and either go down these steps, which are only marginally less slippery, or dive in off the wall closer to the sea.

Kalk Bay 1 is always a few degrees warmer than Kalk Bay 2, and is a great pool for swimming laps or clowning around. For children who aren't yet brave enough to sit on the back wall at Dalebrook and get knocked off by the waves when the tide is high, standing on the little ledge against the back wall of Kalk Bay 1 is a good introduction. Even when the tide is high and the pool gets quite rough, the breaking waves are manageable, showering those standing on that step. To the right corner of the pool, attached to the back wall, is a small set of steps, often covered in urchins, but with giant starfish in nearby corners.

Unfortunately, the southeaster wind howls infamously throughout summer in that part of the world and blows in loads of flotsam and jetsam, including kelp, bluebottles and plastic; the back corner closest to the restaurants is often where this detritus accumulates. The City of Cape Town cleans the pool regularly but the collection of plastic and kelp can't happen fast enough. All swimmers are encouraged to retrieve any plastic they may find.

Kalk Bay 1, off Main Road, Kalk Bay

Size	35 m x 14 m
Swimmability	8
Facilities	Toilets available at the restaurant
Distance from Cape Town CBD	33 km
GPS coordinates	34°07'35.0"S 18°27'02.4"E
Disability access	No wheelchair access into the pools
General access	Free entry (don't be deterred by the signs for the restaurant – the pools are a public space)
Safety	Safe for swimming

Bathing pool, Kalk Bay

20 Kalk Bay 2

Kalk Bay 2, attached to the restaurants surrounding the pools, is the icier of the two pools. It was, when it was built after the first pool, the women's bathing pool. Now both pools are obviously open to all.

This pool is probably the better of the two for training and is frequented by an early-morning group who swim laps. It is sufficiently deep throughout (apart from a large piece of concrete about halfway, against the seaward wall) and has a rocky bottom. It is home to urchins, a variety of fish, anemones, starfish and a range of seaweeds – the variety is astounding when visibility is good. Be careful when you kick off the walls: the urchins usually line this area. When the tide is high, the waves crash over the back wall with a thunderous clap and a massive dramatic vertical spray. At times they are strong enough to knock a grown man off his feet and into the pool – a highly addictive pastime that requires one to climb onto the shared cement wall between the pools and inch one's way carefully along the back wall to wait for the next wave. Not only is this a noble and worthy pastime, it is also amusing for the passersby and diners.

Kalk Bay 2 is highly recommended for early-morning dips when Dalebrook is overrun by swimmers. Stretch out, enjoy the beauty of the bottom as you peer through goggles, and allow your mind to switch off as your body glides through the silken water.

Things to do nearby:

- The pastries at Ohana Beach Cafe in Kalk Bay are completely moreish. Your life will be changed when you eat a pain au chocolat that seemingly contains not only the best chocolate but also more butter than one would think humanly possible to consume.
- Enjoy fresh sushi at Sirocco Café, take in some vinyl DJing on Friday evenings and Sunday afternoons, and people-watch to your heart's content – the restaurant is open to Main Road, where a colourful cast of characters passes.
- Walk to the nearby Kalk Bay harbour to check out the colourful fishing boats, chat with the fishermen and get to know some of the locals – families who have been based in Kalk Bay for generations.
- Book a walking tour of Kalk Bay with Traci Kwaai of the Fisher Child Projekt (visit the Instagram page to learn more). Traci offers a depth of knowledge of the history of Kalk Bay with the authenticity of an adult who grew up in the area and who is deeply connected to the history and stories of its people.

Kalk Bay 2, off Main Road, Kalk Bay

Size	30 m x 20 m
Swimmability	8
Facilities	Toilets available at the restaurant
Distance from Cape Town CBD	33 km
GPS coordinates	34°07'34.55"S 18°27'03.0"E
Disability access	No wheelchair access
General access	Free entry (don't be deterred by the signs for the restaurant – the pools are a public space)
Safety	Safe and family friendly

Busy pools at Kalk Bay 1 & 2, Christmas 1933

Men walking on the walls at Kalk Bay 1 & 2, date unknown

Dalebrook Tidal Pool

21 Dalebrook Tidal Pool

The magic of Dalebrook pool can be found in its mysterious way of evoking in its swimmers the ability to share their life stories with each other unabashedly. In so doing, you become firm friends, if only for the duration of the dip. Some friendships may last longer – it's a lucky packet. Some days one feels quiet companionship and appreciation for other dippers, and on others the weather, sea conditions and visitor energy combine to create a thrilling experience of magical chance encounters.

Dalebrook is accessed from Main Road in Kalk Bay via a cement stairwell, which leads into a subway under the railway. It can be easy to miss given its unmarked entrance, but once you know it's there, it'll draw you in: a stencilled sign above the walkway reads, jubilantly, 'be happy', and it's hard to be anything but happy when visiting this spot. As you emerge from the subway you see the glittering little pool in front of you. Locals adorn the benches and limited seating area along the wall backing onto the railway line side of the pool, drinking coffee and munching pastries from the café across the road. You can drop your swimming gear and towels on the rocks overlooking the pool or find a free spot on the small beach alongside it, and then prepare to brave the icy water.

There are various ways to enter the pool: dive off the wall or go into the water via one of the sets of steps with railings. The pool has a rocky bottom and houses incredibly vibrant sea life: urchins cling to and snails meander across the walls, as yet more unnamed creatures share the pool with revellers. Rising to more or less waist- or shoulder-depth at different points, it is one of the deeper pools on the Cape Peninsula.

The most notable feature of the pool is the large rock in the middle. Children and adults sun themselves on it like lizards as they watch the goings-on around them. At high tide the waves crash over the back wall. Locals enjoy sitting on this wall, waiting to be knocked into the pool, and squeals of laughter can be heard by those brave enough to try this bit of derring-do.

There is limited parking on the road and in a small parking lot 50 m down the road, which makes accessibility tricky during busy periods, like the summer holidays. In summer the pool is quieter at sunrise and sunset, but on warm days when the wind is low, it'll be packed with visitors, so pick your time to visit.

Dalebrook was built in 1903 as part of an illegal private undertaking by Mr F.B. Steer of Douglas Cottage. The initial construction consisted of a seawall and the concreting up of rocks in the east of the pool. Steer decided not to finish the west wall because he found the cost to be too high, especially since it had to adhere to the municipality's regulations. He applied for compensation from the municipality, but his request was denied. The more formal walls were built in 1906. In 1914 the pool was extended towards the sea and the walls were raised. Rocks were also removed from the pool itself, thereby improving the quality of the swimming experience. In the 1950s the council extended the seawall into its now-iconic curve, which more than doubled the pool's size. Bathing boxes were built with a maximum of 20 at the peak. Used by locals and hotel patrons, they were removed in the 1970s.

Things to do nearby:

- Enjoy sushi, pizza, fresh pastries and more from local cafés, or visit the old harbour to see the fishing boats and buy fish and chips. Be sure to visit Chardonnay Deli across the road from Dalebrook – they offer delectable pastries, coffee and free lockers in which to keep your belongings while you swim.
- Browse antique stores and local design boutiques sandwiched between the flower seller and wire artists.
- For the more physically active, there's the option of walking up Echo Valley from Boyes Drive to the Boomslang Caves. Take a torch, wear old clothes and enjoy an easy adventure through the cave, which involves crawling through a tunnel entrance at the start. Be careful not to disturb the bats roosting inside. You can't get lost in the cave: just follow the natural layout and emerge from the other side to spectacular views of the peninsula.

Dalebrook Tidal Pool, off Main Road, Kalk Bay

Size	27 m x 30 m
Swimmability	4
Facilities	Outdoor shower, changing room and toilets
Distance from Cape Town CBD	29 km
GPS coordinates	34°07'26.24"S 18°27'10.81"E
Disability access	No wheelchair access
General access	Free entry
Safety	Safe swimming

Dalebrook Tidal Pool (date unknown)

St James Tidal Pool

22 St James Tidal Pool

In 1886 John Wesley Wells, owner of Botheration Cottage, built the first bathing box at St James, which was then a cove with a rocky bottom, favoured by the women of the time for bathing and dipping, rather than the rough and treacherous sea.

As *The Cape Town Guide* stated in 1897:

> At St. James there is no beach worth mentioning, a pool intended exclusively for ladies' use, has been formed by clearing the rocks away so as to leave a circular space with a sand bottom, girdled round by protecting rocks. There are many other nooks and crannies available for a dip, but the rough rocky bed beneath the bathers' feet, makes the exercise fatiguing and disagreeable. The same remarks in a measure apply to Kalk Bay.

The pool itself was enclosed with back and side walls in 1905, with improvements made in 1923. By 1916 there were 41 bathing boxes and by 1924 the number had increased to 87, with 100 people renting them. In 1923 men's and ladies' amenities were installed next to the Common, which served as an important part of the beach extension. A Marine Research Station was opened on the Common, but no pavilion was ever built at St James. The ladies of the day, and in particular those bathing at St James in 1926, are recorded to have complained about the rocks at the bottom of the pool, which made getting in and out of the water difficult. The same complaints can, at times, be heard by today's visitors.

There is parking on Main Road and in the side streets. The pool is reached via a subway, the entrance of which is next to Folk Café. As you exit the colourfully painted walkway, to the right is the freshwater shower and iconic refurbished bathing boxes standing proudly behind two cement steps. Bathers use them to store their goods and gather for a natter before or after a swim.

St James Tidal Pool is completely submerged during high tide, which makes for an incredibly exhilarating but safe swimming experience. When the tide is lower, you can simply walk from the small sandy beach into the pool, being careful to dodge the rocks. The best way to enter is via the solid cement wall to the right of the pool – you can either dive off into the water towards the back wall or slip in midway along the wall.

Doing lengths isn't great at St James, because the pool very quickly becomes shallow closer to the beach, so most people seem to do widths. The back wall also makes for a fun experience when the waves crash over.

Locals gather at sunrise for morning dips, and young families enjoy the protected aspect of the pool when the southeaster is howling across the rest of the peninsula. Over weekends, visitors flock from all over Cape Town to enjoy the beauty and peace of the pool.

The walls are covered in mussels, sea lettuce, urchins and the odd starfish. The elusive resident octopus has been known to investigate ankle bracelets when bathers stand still long enough.

Things to do nearby:

- Grab a coffee and delectable breakfast at Folk Café next to the pool, which overlooks the railway and sea beyond. The restaurant has a small garden where children can play.
- Sign up for a silent disco and guided immersion via Secret Sunrise, which is also a child-friendly activity.
- Explore the shoreline for sea life. You will find a wide selection of washed-up sea shells.
- To the right of the pool, when the tide is high, a small pool is created from the overflow of the tidal pool, which serves as a toddler's bathing pool.

St James Tidal Pool, off Main Road, St James

Size	35 m x 20 m
Swimmability	5
Facilities	Beach access, freshwater shower, changing rooms and toilets, grassy area perfect for picnics
Distance from Cape Town CBD	28 km
GPS coordinates	34°07'07.65"S 18°27'34.59"E
Disability access	No wheelchair access
General access	Free entry
Safety	Family friendly and safe

St James Tidal Pool, 1913

23 Strandfontein Tidal Pool

The vast Strandfontein pavilion and pool were designed by Vaughn Burns and built between the 1970s and 1980s. Strandfontein and Monwabisi Tidal Pools are the largest man-made tidal pools in South Africa. Strandfontein pool is one of the newest in Cape Town and was constructed during apartheid for use by the local coloured community, who had been displaced from more desirable areas to the Cape Flats.

The pavilion, which separates the parking area from the pool, is enormous but derelict. In its prime, it contained a concert space, shops, restaurants and other facilities to support the large population that visited during the busier summer months.

To reach Strandfontein from Muizenberg, drive along the coastal road (Baden Powell Drive) towards Stellenbosch and, at the first set of traffic lights about 7 km from the traffic circle, turn right. Follow a short tar road to the parking area and drive past the pavilion to the pool. The atmosphere at the pool is eerie: the dilapidated building showcases peculiar architecture and evokes a bygone era – a liminal space yet to be re-envisioned and recreated.

The back wall, a beautiful half-moon curve, leads the eye across the pool to the sea. An attractive sandy beach runs the length of the pool, and a concrete walkway adjoins the pavilion. Entry into the water is from the beach. The pool is deepest close to the back wall but generally shallow, which contributes to its warmth. The local Strandfontein Surf Lifesaving Club trains here and in the sea, which is a short walk from the pool.

Things to do nearby:

- On Sunday mornings fishermen pump for prawns, a meditative tradition to watch.
- Strandfontein lends itself to beautiful photographs – it's mind-blowingly large with incredible angles on the bay and the mountains beyond.

Strandfontein Tidal Pool, New Strandfontein Road, off Baden Powell Drive, Strandfontein

Size	250 m x 100 m
Swimmability	6
Facilities	Toilets, picnic area, parking
Distance from Cape Town CBD	42 km
GPS coordinates	34°05'19.46"S 18°33'17.7"E
Disability access	Partially accessible
General access	Free entry
Safety	Family friendly and safe swimming, best to go in large groups during busy hours

Monwabisi Tidal Pool

24 Monwabisi Tidal Pool

Monwabisi Tidal Pool is the sister pool of Strandfontein Tidal Pool, and is the largest tidal pool in South Africa. Created as a pool and resort for the black population in neighbouring Khayelitsha during the era of apartheid's racial segregation, Monwabisi is a significant but dilapidated site today. High walls were constructed to serve as windbreakers, but owing to the deterioration of the structures, they have become a safety hazard. Despite its current state of serious disrepair, locals still frequent the resort during the summer months. However, the pool, originally designed to protect bathers from the rough surrounding seas, is no longer considered a safe place as a result of rampant crime.

Architect Graham Parker designed Monwabisi for the City of Cape Town, and it was constructed in 1986. Positioned between Wolfgat Nature Reserve and the Macassar dunes, the resort benefits from natural barriers, with white limestone and calcrete cliffs on both sides of the beach. This geographical setup made it a favourable location for a separate amenity during apartheid, allowing for the easy containment of people. The cliffs and dunes, along with the ocean, formed a natural boundary. The entire resort area is fenced along the coastline of False Bay, preventing movement into the fynbos and dune area beyond.

According to a *Cape Times* report dated 6 January 2010, as quoted in a thesis by Vincent Bezuidenhout, 'The treacherous sea at the Monwabisi resort near Khayelitsha claimed three more lives yesterday'. This incident was part of a series of reports designating the resort as one of the most perilous beaches in the region, with one record indicating five drownings in a single day. The construction of a breakwater intended to create a calm cove seems to be a contributing factor. The accumulation of sand in this area has resulted in an artificial beach next to the rock pool, with strong currents. According to the NSRI, there were more than 50 drownings at Monwabisi between 1990 and 2005. In recent years there have been lifeguards on duty and better control over the number of people able to enter at any time, which should make the resort safer.

Monwabisi is a culturally significant space. It is often used by religious groups for ceremonies, services and baptisms. During summer holidays Monwabisi (which means 'bringing joy' in Xhosa) is the nearest swimming spot for the population of Khayelitsha, one of the largest townships in South Africa, and it provides relief, refreshment and respite from the often extremely difficult conditions in which residents here live. Though the facilities are badly run-down, the pool and its surrounding areas still provide a welcome service for residents of the area, who often have to walk many hot kilometres to this coastal refuge.

Things to do nearby:

- Visit the Village House restaurant for an authentic African experience, complete with traditional cuisine and warm Xhosa hospitality.

- In August after the big rains, enjoy the beautiful endangered vegetation along the road through the tiny cliffside Wolfgat Nature Reserve, home to rare birds and reptiles.
- Visit the 18 Gangster Museum in Khayelitsha for intriguing exhibits on the impacts of gang life.
- Take a township tour of the historically important Khayelitsha township.

Monwabisi Tidal Pool, off Baden Powell Drive, Khayelitsha

Size	150 m x 240 m
Swimmability	4
Facilities	Braai and picnic facilities, toilets and kiosks
Distance from Cape Town CBD	36 km
GPS coordinates	34°04'27.45"S 18°41'16.24"E
Disability access	No wheelchair access
General access	Entrance fee in summer
Safety	Safe swimming but generally not safe owing to crime

Strand Tidal Pool

25 Strand Tidal Pool

Strand Tidal Pool could easily be missed, nondescript as it is. Its gentle half-moon shape and curving back wall offer protection from the sea. At high tide, the pool is all but invisible, but is situated right on Strand Beach with views of the Hottentots Holland Mountains in the distance and the picturesque, uninterrupted beach.

This little pool is 500 m before the Strand Pavilion if you're driving from Cape Town. Park on Beach Road close to Murray Street, and you'll find it across at the beach. The pool, which has a soft sandy entrance, is great for young children and parents who just want to relax on the sand without having to worry about big waves. It's not a pool for long training swims, but little dips make it a wonderful and safe place on a summer afternoon.

Things to do nearby:

- Walk 500 m towards the mountains and you'll come across the Strand Pavilion, which, architecturally, harks back to resort towns like Brighton in England and their large pavilions.
- Visit the historic and charming Bikini Beach tucked into a corner of Gordon's Bay next to the harbour.
- Visit Morgenster Estate and indulge in an extra-virgin olive oil tasting with international award-winning olive oils produced on the farm. Morgenster is on Vergelegen Avenue, which is on your way into the Cape Winelands, and well worth the visit.
- Bikini Beach Books is a well-known bookstore, offering everything from bodice rippers to business books.
- Ooskus Fisheries in Gordon's Bay has excellent fish and chips. Get a takeaway and sit on the beachfront at Gordon's Bay for sundowners.
- Drive to the top of Sir Lowry's Pass and park to the right of the road where there's a lookout point with wonderful views all the way to Table Mountain. Be warned, though, that when the wind is blowing strongly, standing outside your vehicle on the edge of the mountain can be dangerous.

Strand Tidal Pool, Beach Road, Strand

Size	136 m x 45 m
Swimmability	2
Facilities	Restaurants across the road, no ablutions or braai facilities
Distance from Cape Town CBD	49 km
GPS coordinates	34°06'59.51"S 18°49'25.24"E
Disability access	No wheelchair access
General access	Free entry
Safety	Safe swimming

Harmony Park Tidal Pool

26 Harmony Park Tidal Pool

Harmony Park was built in early 1991 and 1992 by the Planning Partnership and Interplan Architects for what was then, during apartheid, the Department of Coloured Affairs and it was allocated for coloured use only. In August 1989, Archbishop Desmond Tutu had defied orders from the apartheid government and led hundreds of protestors to picnic at the 'whites only' Strand Beach, less than 2 km away from Harmony Park Resort in Strand. Tutu declared, 'We have proved these are God's beaches.'

Harmony Park must be one of the most architecturally interesting and beautifully designed pools in South Africa, with whimsical curves and a high breakwater back wall. A wooden pier juts boldly through the centre of the pool towards the sea and offers lovely views of the swimmers and pool below. Small cement islands offer mermaid-like basking between laps around the channels that arc through the pool. The shallow end, closest to the beach, is great for small children, but there is also a protected children's pool. For those wanting rigorous training swims, this is a great pool for distance, and when the waves break over the wall the choppy water can add an additional challenge. The water is consistently deep, above head-height, for most of the way around the channels. Despite how intentional the design was, the pool feels slightly abandoned and wild, with uninterrupted views of the sea beyond.

There is frequent evidence of otter activity in the area, and the quiet stretches of beach and unkept flora nearby are a haven for birds and some mammals.

Brave teenagers jump or attempt various dives off the pier but I wouldn't recommend it. The margin for error is slim and the water is dark with poor visibility, so there's no telling what you could land on. In summer, it's incredibly busy, but in autumn there are only a handful of swimmers, mostly locals, and the sense of space is incredible.

Harmony Park Tidal Pool, Flow Street, Strand

Size	150 m x 60 m but, given its unique configuration, a full length is 400 m
Swimmability	9
Facilities	Parking, picnic and braai areas, lifeguards and toilets
Distance from Cape Town CBD	52 km
GPS coordinates	34°08'22.51"S 18°50'45.63"E
Disability access	Wheelchair access
General access	Free entry
Safety	Safe swimming

Sparks Bay Tidal Pool

27 Sparks Bay Tidal Pool

Clarence Drive, celebrated as one of the most picturesque routes in the province, winds around the Hottentots Holland Mountains, providing stunning views from Gordon's Bay to Betty's Bay. As you leave Gordon's Bay, be sure to adhere to the speed limit, and be vigilant for baboons crossing the road. You will soon find yourself in a vast expanse of unspoilt natural beauty that extends for kilometres.

Keep an eye out for the well-marked turnoff to Sparks Bay Tidal Pool. Although navigating through the campsite and around to the right for parking may be somewhat confusing, the pool beckons invitingly once you've found your spot. A brief stroll down a sandy road reveals an enchanting, expansive and refreshingly cold tidal pool.

Enter the pool either from the sandy beach or down the steps and, if you're feeling adventurous, perhaps even off the wall (pay attention to the varying depth throughout the pool – the shallowest end is near the beach!). Beware of urchins – this cannot be stressed enough. The pool boasts spectacular sea life, with urchins aplenty, and visitors often spot baboons and cormorants in the area. This is, without a doubt, the number one pool in which to wear booties!

Stretch out and savour the spaciousness of this vast pool, even during busy times. In the summer months, lifeguards are on duty. There is no shade, so bring an umbrella. Owing to its remote nature, it isn't the best-maintained pool, and sometimes there is broken glass nearby. The beach is shelly, not sandy. If you choose to camp nearby, this is a lovely spot from which to watch the sunset.

Things to do nearby:

- For surfers and bodyboarders, when all the surf is gone there are still some good waves at a spot called Caves just below the cliffs.
- Crystal Pools is a well-known series of natural freshwater pools located up a gorge closer to Gordon's Bay. In order to hike and then swim this route, you need to book online and purchase permits, which a guard checks at the gate.
- Swim at the Palmiet River a short drive away. Park just on the other side of the bridge that you cross a few kilometres before entering Kleinmond and make your way down to the river. This is a welcome stop on a hot daytrip.
- Visit the Harold Porter National Botanical Gardens in Betty's Bay, where a few more beautiful swims await.
- There is a penguin colony at Betty's Bay.

Sparks Bay Tidal Pool, Clarence Drive, Gordon's Bay

Size	100 m x 40 m
Swimmability	8
Facilities	Braai and picnic facilities, very basic and sometimes broken/unclean ablutions
Distance from Cape Town CBD	69 km
GPS coordinates	34°14'51.89"S 18°51'15.73"E
Disability access	No wheelchair access
General access	Free entry
Safety	Safe swimming

OVERBERG

The Overberg is nestled beyond the formidable Hottentots Holland Mountains. This expansive area stretches along the southern coast of the Western Cape, forming a picturesque boundary between the Cape Peninsula to the west and the renowned Garden Route to the east. Contrary to popular belief, the Atlantic Ocean meets the Indian Ocean not at Cape Point, but at Cape Agulhas, which is in the Overberg district and is also the southernmost tip of Africa.

Deep within the folds of the Overberg region lies the Kogelberg Biosphere Reserve, a gem acknowledged and endorsed by UNESCO. Here, a rich tapestry of flowering plants flourishes, boasting a remarkable diversity exclusive to the fynbos biome.

With its majestic mountain ranges, vibrant fynbos landscapes, expansive wheat and canola fields and quaint towns, the area is also famous for whale-watching and boasts a notable architectural legacy.

Jan Rabie Tidal Pool

28 Jan Rabie Tidal Pool

Jan Rabie Tidal Pool takes its name from the prolific Afrikaans writer Jan Rabie, who lived nearby. Legend has it that he and his wife, artist Marjorie Wallace, would visit it for a dip, sometimes twice a day.

It is ideal for swimming and sunset views and is best visited at higher tide; however, caution is advised during high tide owing to crashing waves. There are several access points and a few rocks from which to jump.

From a design perspective, it must be one of the most interesting, and is certainly the most inspired, of all the pools in this region. Some walls were constructed around a 1–2-m-deep natural cove, but allow for natural flow of the tides in and out of the pool. Because there is quite a large swathe of rocks between the pool and the sea, the pool is relatively well protected from kelp washing into it. The pool is shaped like a seven, with a shallower long stretch, about 7 m wide, leading from a broken cement walkway, with a handrail, to a grassy patch near the car park. If you enter the water here, take care and wear booties because there are many urchins and sharp rocks along the bottom. Swim towards the cleft between the rocks on the sea side of the pool and you'll enter an incredible 3-m-deep channel bordered by black rock, with a wall to one side of it. Fresh water enters with the change of the tides, and even in summer the temperature is remarkably fresh. The shallower section near the beach is good for bobbing about, and the deeper cove perpendicular to it is lovely for stretching out if there aren't too many other people around. Its deep, cool waters are welcoming and refreshing. A broken concrete wall is a useful place to stow your clothes and towel while you swim, its harshness a stark contrast to the soft natural beauty of the pool and its shiny rocks.

The pool is popular with sunset dippers and picnickers on the lawn. The view beyond the pool across Walker Bay must be one of the most beautiful in the world.

Things to do nearby:

- Do a two-part sunrise tidal pool hop and visit nearby Davie's Pool, which is a short walk away.
- Riposo Italian Eatery offers authentic Italian pizzas, which are to die for!
- Bring a picnic and enjoy the splendour of the surrounding natural beauty.

Jan Rabie Tidal Pool, Albatross Street, Onrus River, Onrus

Size	The pool can be separated into two zones, both 45 m x 7 m
Swimmability	5
Facilities	Camping
Distance from Cape Town CBD	114 km
GPS coordinates	34°25'08.01"S 19°09'47.18"E
Disability access	No wheelchair access
General access	Free entry
Safety	Safe for swimming

29 Davie's Pool

A 500-m stroll from Jan Rabie Tidal Pool brings you to Davie's Pool, formerly known as the Mermaid's Pool, constructed by David Jonathan Davies. Surrounded by rocks that provide protection from crashing waves, it is essentially a natural pool, with a cement walkway and handrail offering support to swimmers. While it is best to visit during mid-tide, swimmers can be found at all hours of the day.

Davie's is a popular spot at sunset, with children and adults lounging about, enjoying picnics and exploring the small rock pools around the tidal pool. The entrance to Onrus Caravan Park adjoins the lawn next to the pool, offering campers easy access without a lengthy walk around the perimeter fence.

The meandering walkway along the pool features beautiful ceramic plaques honouring those who loved the area and swimming in the pool. This local initiative is tastefully executed and maintained by the community. A kiosk on the grassy verge called Coffee at Davies Pool, provides delectable takeaway cappuccinos, milkshakes, ice creams and iced coffees. Outdoor exercise equipment is spread along this grassy area, creating a workout space with a breathtaking view. A mosaic by artist Marie Peacey, crafted in memory of her mother, adorns the wall of the immaculate ablution facilities.

Davie's Pool is an excellent swimming location, even during high tide and inclement weather, thanks to its level bottom and protection from breaking waves. It offers endless hours of enjoyment for people of all ages, especially those interested in exploring various marine life forms. Wearing booties is advisable here owing to the substantial presence of sea urchins.

Things to do nearby:

- Take the Rotary Way drive to the Lookout point on the hill overlooking Hermanus.
- Hang out at Milk on the Beach on Onrus Beach.

Davie's Pool, 34 Krige St, Onrus River, Onrus

Size	60 m x 25 m
Swimmability	3 at high tide, otherwise 1
Facilities	Large playground, coffee kiosk, ablution facilities
Distance from Cape Town CBD	115 km
GPS coordinates	34°25'01.05"S 19°10'03.17"E
Disability access	No wheelchair access, but a handrail offers some support into the water
General access	Free
Safety	Safe swimming

30 Ficks Pool

Parking for Ficks Pool is just off Marine Drive in a small lot. Follow the signs directing you down the steps to the pool. Similar to Kalk Bay 1 & 2, there is a restaurant around Ficks Pool, and many older visitors reminisce about a time when the pool existed without this addition, which has significantly decreased the open space around it. Sunrise visits to the pool are ideal – it has a serene atmosphere, with only a few people taking a dip. As summer progresses, the sun's warmth intensifies by 9 a.m., signalling the opportune time to leave.

Ficks Pool is a beloved destination, offering a lot despite its small size. You can get into the water via the somewhat weathered steps with a handrail, next to cement slabs that now serve as sunbathing spots. It is easier to enter the pool by walking to the left around it, through the open-air restaurant, and descending the steps, with only a few rocks to navigate around. The more adventurous walk along the enclosing wall leads you to a spot to jump in (there are some rocks, so this must be done with caution). The rocks to the right of the pool present more challenging jumps.

Residents of the pool include silvery fish, larger grey fish and an octopus that has been spotted a few times around sunrise. During weekends, the pool is predictably busy. The restaurant opens at 11 a.m., offering tapas, wine and soft drinks, but its prices position it as an exclusive spot catering to tourists and retirees. Nevertheless, it provides arguably the best view of the pool and the ocean beyond.

The water in Ficks Pool is always fresh, with no issues of stagnant water posing safety concerns. During the roaring twenties, Hermanus had just one governmental institution for the education of its youth – the quaintly named Klipskool. At the helm was Mr J.J. Fick, who, together with his family, resided in the house perched about the swimming *gat*. Economic hardships cast a shadow over the town, rendering weekends and holidays devoid of ample entertainment for the younger children of the area.

While the sandy beaches of Mossel River and Voëlklip beckoned to beachgoers, the absence of recreational diversions within the town itself was palpable. It was Mr Fick who sought to redress this imbalance, petitioning the council to carve out a swimming oasis in front of his home. The endeavour demanded the dynamiting of rocky precipices, the removal of a prominent craggy outcrop, and the erection of a sturdy concrete barricade, later complemented by rudimentary wooden changing quarters. In 1933, Ficks Pool made its debut, swiftly capturing the town's collective imagination.

An alternative genesis tale traces its roots to Josias Servaas Fick, a long-standing denizen of the Caledon region in the late 19th century. It is said that he established a daily ritual of morning swims at his holiday residence, giving rise to the moniker Fick se Gat, which, over time, metamorphosed into the anglicised appellation of Ficks Pool.

Come 1965, a substantial refurbishment unfolded, as diligent municipal hands toiled to rid the pool bed of loose debris. Concurrently, the Rotary Club rallied funds to extend the seaward perimeter, elongating the pool's dimensions to an impressive 50 m while also elevating its stature.

The endeavours undertaken transformed Ficks Pool into a magnet for both residents and tourists, drawing them in with its allure. With a rich tapestry of stories woven into its past, the pool has become not only a hub of leisure but also a cornerstone of Hermanus's cultural legacy.

Ficks Pool was a regular haunt for General Jan Smuts, who frequented Hermanus, where his sister lived. He started his day with a swim at the pool, following it with breakfast, work, a brief rest and a walk up the local mountain behind Northcliff before supper.

Things to do nearby:

- Take a stroll along the famous Cliff Path, which meanders for kilometres.
- Do some coasteering along the cliffs – cliff jumps of up to 15 m await! If you're inexperienced or don't know the area, look up a reputable local company to guide you and provide safety gear.
- Take a jog up the steps to Hoy's Koppie in the middle of town to get the lay of the land.
- Organise a visit to the South African National Space Agency's magnetic observatory – a fascinating facility.
- Take a wander through the Fernkloof Nature Reserve, with its incredible range of fynbos.
- Visit the quaint old harbour, which is also a fantastic swimming spot.

Ficks Pool, off Marine Drive, Hermanus

Size	27 m x 20 m
Swimmability	5
Facilities	Surrounded by a Spanish tapas and wine bar
Distance from Cape Town CBD	121 km
GPS coordinates	34°25'21.49"S 19°14'8.96"E
Disability access	No wheelchair access
General access	Free entry
Safety	Safe swimming

Ficks Pool, T. D. Ravenscroft

Marine Pool

31 Marine Pool

Once dubbed Bientang se Baaigat by the townsfolk, the Marine Pool harboured a connection to Bientang, believed to the be the final representative of the Khoisan community in Hermanus, and said to dwell in a nearby cave.

During the vibrant era of the 1920s, the Marine Hotel garnered widespread acclaim, serving as a magnet for affluent and noble figures. Among its distinguished guests were Prince Arthur of Connaught, a grandson of Queen Victoria, and Sir William Hoy, a perennial patron for numerous years.

Access to the pool is via the Cliff Path, involving a descent down steep steps. This route is not advisable for individuals with mobility challenges. The pool provides a secure swimming environment, but swim shoes or booties are recommended owing to urchins and sharp rocks. At low tide, the pool becomes an excellent spot for snorkelling, offering a captivating view of the ocean and its surroundings. The pool's location, sheltered from crashing waves, makes it a safe option for children. Its visibility from the hotel and roads further enhances its safety features.

The pool is deep enough – 1.5 m along the wall – to do some lengths, and just shallow enough at its edges and around the rocks for children to splash about comfortably.

There is a grassy patch just above the pool and rocks to the left where fishermen like to gather at sunrise. The steps leading up to the hotel are used for exercise purposes by those who want to raise their heart rate. Most of us, however, simply enjoy the pleasures of the cool water, big blue skies and yet another pastry and coffee. Oskars Café & Bakery offers a selection of excellent pastries and coffee.

Things to do nearby:

- Hermanus is famous for its whale-watching. You can do this from the comfort of a restaurant near the old harbour, or via a boat operated by a professional tour company. The best time to watch whales is between June and November each year.
- The Hemel-en-Aarde Valley (Heaven and Earth Valley) is a meandering route through the rolling mountains behind Hermanus. Besides the lovely drive, it offers a selection of wine farms where you can stop for a bite to eat and taste some of the local cultivars. Some of the most popular farms are Creation Wines, which boasts a fantastic view, and Hamilton Russell Vineyards.
- The Hermanus Country Market takes place every Saturday from 9 a.m.– 2 p.m., and offers an array of delicious foods and crafts, from wooden carvings of whales to handmade jewellery. The focus is on natural, fresh and locally produced foods, and supporting the local community.

- Hemingways Bookshop is a charming antiquarian and used bookshop. Pop in and you're sure to leave with a number of interesting books, after having enjoyed a conversation with some of the knowledgeable staff. If you're looking for newer holiday reads pop into the Bookmark, which is situated conveniently close to Oskars.

Marine Pool, Cliff Path, off Marine Drive, Hermanus

Size	70 m x 30 m
Swimmability	5
Facilities	Toilets and freshwater showers
Distance from Cape Town CBD	121 km
GPS coordinates	34°25'04.89"S 19°14'46.67"E
Disability access	No wheelchair access
General access	Free entry
Safety	Safe swimming

32 Sonop Sononder Pool

Nestled just below the Sonop Sononder lookout spot off the Cliff Path, beyond Sievers Point, is Sonop Sononder Pool. Resembling Cape Point's Venus Pool, it boasts a natural setting with just enough depth for a refreshing dip, allowing visitors to bob in the water as waves rush in over the adjacent bank of rocks. A charming sandy beach borders the pool, accompanied by little rock pools that provide delightful exploration for children.

While it is not advisable to access during high tide, Sonop Sononder is a hidden gem at low tide. Abundant with sea life, this little oasis is a worthwhile excursion off the beaten track.

To reach the pool, park at the small sandy parking lot off Kwaaiwater Road. A short walk towards Hermanus proper will lead you to a small sign that reads Sonop Sononder. The little natural pool is just below this, sheltered by the rocks.

Sonop Sononder, Cliff Path, Hermanus

Size	5 m x 5 m
Swimmability	1
Facilities	No ablutions
Distance from Cape Town CBD	123 km
GPS coordinates	34°24'52.01"S 19°15'01.63"E
Disability access	No wheelchair access
General access	Free entry
Safety	Safe swimming

Gansbaai Tidal Pool

33 Gansbaai Tidal Pool

Situated about 40 km from Hermanus, Gansbaai and Kleinbaai mark the end of the Overberg pools. Built in the 1950s, these smaller pools are a haven for swimming amidst the shark-infested waters just beyond their walls. Not only known for their fishing traditions and working harbour, Gansbaai and Kleinbaai are famous for the great white shark population around Dyer Island, located just off the coast.

Accessed via a small dirt road, Gansbaai Tidal Pool has limited parking and braai facilities. Nestled next to tall reeds on a grassy lawn, the pool is long but not very deep, with insufficient drainage during low tide. Popular among locals on weekends and less frequented during the week, it exudes a remote ambiance despite nearby houses overlooking it. It is advisable to wear booties because there is broken glass in places.

The small children's pool is fed by a freshwater spring, which ensures it is consistently full. While the view of the ocean and surrounding rock pools is spectacular, spotting a whale might require binoculars.

Things to do nearby:

- The coastline in this area is extraordinary, with wonderful pathways, hidden beaches and caves. De Kelders (The Cellars), a tiny district of Gansbaai, has a series of caves in the sea cliffs, including Klipgat Cave where archaeologists found evidence of human habitation going back 80 000 years. Take the time to explore and imagine what life was like here for the original inhabitants tens of thousands of years ago.
- Book a retreat at the deeply relaxing Bodhi Khaya, a long-time favourite for those who seek a deeper calm.
- Book a cheese tasting at the Klein River Cheese Farmstead near Stanford.
- A beer tasting is a novelty at Birkenhead Brewery near Stanford.
- Visit the ancient forest of Platbos, known to be one of the oldest, southernmost Afromontane forests in Africa. Here you will find trees estimated to be over a thousand years old and a variety of birds to tick off the list.
- Book yourself a stay at the luxurious Grootbos Private Nature Reserve, with a view over the Platbos forest.

Gansbaai Tidal Pool, Gansbaai, Overberg

Size	50 m x 10 m (freshwater kiddies' pool 4 m x 4 m)
Swimmability	1
Facilities	Braai facilities
Distance from Cape Town CBD	164 km
GPS coordinates	34°34'29.59"S 19°20'47.56"E
Disability access	No wheelchair access
General access	Free
Safety	Very safe

34 Kleinbaai Tidal Pool

Kleinbaai Tidal Pool is perched on the edge of a large lawned area with braai facilities and playground equipment. A man-made island is perfect for jumping into the pool when it is full.

You can find ample parking in a lot at the end of Kabeljou Street, or along its length. The pool is easy to spot across the gently sloping lawn. Access to the pool is from the beach, which is particularly shelly. At high tide it's suitable for swimming a few short lengths, but it isn't an ideal pool in which to really stretch out for a training swim. Kelp has a tendency to collect in the pool and irregular removal means the pool can sometimes be quite swampy. At best, the pool is chest-deep.

The surrounding coastline makes for an excellent afternoon meander and if the tide is high and the conditions right this pool will provide a welcome dip. From the pool you can see the big shark-cage diving boats that leave from a slipway nearby for Dyer Island, about 20 km out to sea. Laze about in this pool safe in the knowledge that all predatory fish are far away.

Things to do nearby:

- Visit the African Penguin and Seabird Sanctuary. It is a cutting-edge establishment that aims to offer a haven for indigenous marine avian species. Here, injured, ailing or distressed bids find solace and care, undergoing treatment and rehabilitation in their journey back to health.
- Pearly Beach Horse Trails offers beginner and experienced riders the chance to experience the coastline by horseback. Booking is essential.
- Dyer Island Cruises offers a boat tour of the marine big five – whales, dolphins, seals, penguins and great white sharks. The tour takes you all the way to Dyer Island and is family safe.

Kleinbaai Tidal Pool, off Kabeljou Street, Kleinbaai

Size	50 m x 30 m
Swimmability	3
Facilities	Toilets, braai facilities, play area
Distance from Cape Town CBD	168 km
GPS coordinates	34°37'05.05"S 19°21'09.17"E
Disability access	No wheelchair access
General access	Free, unfenced
Safety	Very safe

Gear for tidal pool swimming

To help you make the most of your tidal pool adventure, below is a list of essential gear and some recommended options.

- **Bathing suit:** Do choose a very comfortable swimming costume that allows freedom of movement.
- **Swimming cap:** A cap is a good idea if the water is particularly cold, or if you want to keep your hair dry.
- **Earplugs:** Cold-water exposure can cause a condition known as 'surfer's ear', where bone growths develop in the ear canal in response to repeated exposure to cold water and wind. Earplugs can help to maintain balance by preventing water from affecting the inner ear, which is crucial for swimming efficiently.
- **Wetsuit:** Depending on the water temperature, you might opt for a wetsuit for added warmth.
- **Rash guard or dive skin:** Protect your skin from abrasions and the sun's rays with a rash guard or dive skin. These garments also offer some insulation.
- **Water shoes:** Sturdy water shoes (booties) with good traction protect your feet from sharp rocks, urchins and rough surfaces, and give you grip in slippery areas.
- **Goggles:** Clear vision underwater is essential for observing marine life and navigating tidal pools. Choose goggles that fit snugly and have a good seal.
- **Snorkel and mask:** A snorkel-and-mask combo allows you to observe underwater environments, spot marine creatures and explore the tidal pools without having to constantly lift your head for air.
- **Swim fins:** Swim fins (flippers) can improve your mobility and help you move more efficiently through the water.
- **Sunscreen:** The African sun can be harsh throughout the year. Apply a marine-friendly, waterproof sunscreen with a high SPF to shield your skin from the sun's UV rays, especially if you'll be spending a significant amount of time outdoors.
- **Waterproof bag or dry pouch:** Keep your belongings, such as keys, phone and snacks, safe in a waterproof bag or dry pouch.
- **Appropriate clothing and towel:** Have dry clothes and a towel ready for after your swim to help you warm up.

- **Underwater camera or GoPro:** Capture the beauty of the tidal pools and the fascinating marine life with an underwater camera or a GoPro.
- **Safety gear:** Depending on the specific conditions of the tidal pool area, consider carrying a safety buoy, whistle or other signalling device.
- **Educational material:** If you're interested in marine life, consider bringing along a field guide or app to help with identifying the species you encounter.

First-aid kit

Open-water swimmers and their tidal pool swimming counterparts tend to take safety extremely seriously: when something goes wrong, it can go badly wrong, and you want to ensure you're prepared for this unfortunate eventuality.

It's important to consider how extensive the kit might need to be, depending on what you plan to do. However, I'd advise being overprepared rather than finding yourself in a pickle. I have included what I consider to be essential items, but the list is not exhaustive. Most swimmers I know keep their first-aid kit in the boot of their car or in a separate pouch in their swimming bag.

Store all the items below in a waterproof container to protect them from water damage.

- **Antiseptic wipes and solution:** For cleaning wounds and preventing infection.
- **Sterile gauze pads and adhesive bandages:** Essential for covering and protecting minor cuts, scrapes and abrasions.
- **Adhesive tape and plasters:** Useful for securing dressings.
- **Small scissors:** For cutting tape, bandages or clothing.
- **Tweezers:** Essential for removing urchin quills or other objects from under the skin.
- **Pain medication:** Useful for minor aches and pains, stings or pricks from marine life.
- **Compact emergency blanket:** Provides warmth and protection from hypothermia in case of excessive cold-water exposure.
- **Personal medications:** If you have any specific medical conditions, include your medication in the first-aid kit.
- **CPR mask:** In case of a medical emergency requiring CPR, a CPR mask will provide protection and help with breathing.

Don't forget to replenish your kit if you use something when you're out and about. I've always found plasters and antiseptic solution important to have on hand.

As your swimming progresses, consider taking a first-aid course to deepen and expand your ability to respond to emergencies.

Bibliography

Akhalbey, Francis. 'Defiant Desmond Tutu Led Hundreds of Protesters to Picnic at a Whites-only Beach on this Day in 1989'. Face2Face Africa, 2019. Available: https://face2faceafrica.com/article/defiant-desmond-tutu-led-hundreds-of-protesters-to-picnic-at-a-whites-only-beach-on-this-day-in-1989-photos [18 February 2024].

Bank, Leslie. 'Frontiers of Freedom: Race, Landscape and Nationalism in the Coastal Cultures of South Africa'. *Anthropology Southern Africa*, 38: 3–4, 248–268, 2015. Available: https://doi.org/10.1080/23323256.2015.1088790 [17 February 2024].

Berman, M.G., Jonides, J. and Kaplan, S. 'The Cognitive Benefits of Interacting with Nature'. *Psychological Science*, 19(12): 1207–1212, 2008. Available: https://pubmed.ncbi.nlm.nih.gov/19121124/ [2 February 2024].

Berner, I., Hofmann, B. and Spangenberg, K. 'The Development of Monwabisi. A Situational Study: Evaluation report', 2004.

Bezuidenhout, Vincent. 'Separate Amenities: Topographics of Recreational Spaces in South Africa' (Master's thesis). Cape Town, University of Cape Town, 2011. Available: https://www.academia.edu/8433016/Separate_Amenities_Topographics_of_Recreational_Spaces_in_South_Africa [21 April 2024].

Biodiversity and Tourism on the Cape West Coast. West Coast Way, 2017. Available: https://www.westcoastway.co.za/biodiversity-tourism-cape-west-coast/ [20 April 2024].

Bosman, D.E. and Scholtz, D.J.P. 'A Survey of Man-made Tidal Swimming Pools along the South African Coast', *Coastal Engineering*, 1982. Available: https://ascelibrary.org/doi/10.1061/9780872623736.152 [2 February 2024].

Caboz, Jay. 'Feel Good: Cape Town Tidal Pools Will Now Be Cleaned in Eco-friendly Ways', *News24*, 5 March 2020. Available: https://www.news24.com/news24/bi-archive/cape-town-tidal-pools-will-now-be-cleaned-using-eco-friendly-methods-2020-3 [19 April 2024].

Cape Peninsula Holiday Haunts. Cape Town: Issued Under the Auspices of the Corporation of the City of Capetown [*sic*] and the General Manager, South African Railways Publishers, 1918.

The Cape Town Guide. Cape Town: Dennis Edwards & Co., 1897. Available: https://repository.up.ac.za/handle/2263/18065 [17 February 2024].

Durrheim, Kevin and Dixon, John. 'The Role of Place and Metaphor in Racial Exclusion: South Africa's Beaches as Sites of Shifting Racialization', *Ethnic and Racial Studies*, 24(3): 433–450, 2001. Available: https://www.tandfonline.com/doi/abs/10.1080/01419870020036738 [31 January 2024].

'5 Pillars Project Report'. Waves for Change, 2023. Available: https://waves-for-change.org/5-pillars-project-report/ [17 February 2024].

Franke, Hillary A. 'Toxic Stress: Effects, Prevention and Treatment'. *Children (Basel)*, 1(3): 309–402, 2014. Available: https://www.ncbi.nlm.nih.gov/pmc/articles/PMC4928741/ [2 February 2024].

Gasson, Barrie. 'Kalk Bay Historical Association Bulletin No. 16'. Cape Town: The Kalk Bay Historical Association, 2012. Available: https://www.kbha.co.za/BULLETINS/16/mobile/index.html [17 February 2024].

Gasson, Barrie. 'Kalk Bay Historical Association Bulletin No. 17'. Cape Town: The Kalk Bay Historical Association, 2013. Available: https://www.kbha.co.za/BULLETINS/17/mobile/index.html [17 February 2024].

Goitom, Hannibal. 'On This Day: Desegregation of South Africa's Beaches'. Library of Congress Blogs, 2015. Available: https://blogs.loc.gov/law/2015/11/on-this-day-desegregation-of-south-african-beaches/ [16 February 2024].

Hartig, T., Mang, M. and Evans, G.W. 'Restorative Effects of Natural Environment Experiences'. *Environment and Behavior*, 23(1): 3–26, 1991. Available: https://journals.sagepub.com/doi/10.1177/0013916591231001 [2 February 2024].

'Hermanus Cliff Path: What's in a Name?' Hermanus History Society, 2018. Available: https://www.hermanus-history-society.co.za/2018/09/19/hermanus-cliff-path-whats-in-a-name/ [17 February 2024].

Hine, P., Sealy, J., Halkett, D. and Hart, T. 'Antiquity of Stone-Walled Tidal Fish Traps on the Cape Coast, South Africa'. *The South African Archaeological Bulletin*, 65(191): 35–44, June 2010. Available: jstor.org/stable/40985509 [17 February 2024].

Kaplan, R. and Kaplan, S. *The Experience of Nature: A Psychological Perspective*. Cambridge: Cambridge University Press, 1989.

Kretzmann, Steve. 'Sewage on the Seashore: Here's What's Causing Cape Town's Beach Closures'. *GroundUp*, 31 January 2023. Available: https://groundup.org.za/article/sewage-on-the-seashore-spoils-cape-town-holiday-season/ [19 April 2024].

Lee, Robin. 'The Colourful History of Fick's Pool'. Hermanus History Society, 2017. Available: https://www.hermanus-history-society.co.za/2017/12/22/969/ [19 February 2024].

Love, Christopher. *A Social History of Swimming in England, 1800–1918*. London: Routledge, 2007.

Maas, J., van Dillen, S.M., Verheij, R.A. and Groenewegen, P.P. 'Social Contacts as a Possible Mechanism behind the Relation between Green Space and Health'. *Health & Place*, 15(2): 586–595, 2009. Available: https://pubmed.ncbi.nlm.nih.gov/19022699/ [2 February 2024].

'Mental Health Matters', *The Lancet*. Elsevier, 8(11), November 2020. Available: https://www.thelancet.com/journals/langlo/article/PIIS2214-109X(20)30432-0/fulltext [2 February 2024].

'Mental State of the World, 2021'. *Sapiens Labs*, 2022. Available: https://sapienlabs.org/wp-content/uploads/2022/03/Mental-State-of-the-World-Report-2021.pdf. [2 February 2024].

Nichols, Wallace J. *Blue Mind: How Water Makes You Happier, More Connected and Better at What You Do*. London: Little, Brown, 2014.

Omond, Roger. *The Apartheid Handbook*. Middlesex: Harmondsworth, 1985.

Park, Michael. 'Cape Racial Reform: Open Beaches Unnerve Many South Africans', *Los Angeles Times*, 11 February 1985. Available: https://www.latimes.com/archives/la-xpm-1985-02-11-mn-4294-story.html [31 January 2024].

Raymond, L. 'Monwabisi Beach Too Dangerous, Says NSRI'. *IOL*, 2005 Available: http://www.iol.co.za/news/south-africa/monwabisi-beach-too-dangerous-says-nsri-1.247919 [18 February 2024].

Rogerson J.M. 'Kicking Sand in the Face of Apartheid: Segregated Beaches in South Africa'. In: Rogatka, K. and Szymańska, D. (eds.), *Bulletin of Geography. Socio-economic Series*, No. 35. Toruń: Nicolaus Copernicus University, pp. 93–109, 2017. Available: https://www.bulletinofgeography.umk.pl/35_2017/07_Rogerson.pdf [31 January 2024].

Sachs, Albie. 'The Secret Weapon of Maiden's Cove for All', *Daily Maverick*, 4 September 2018. Available: https://www.dailymaverick.co.za/article/2018-09-04-the-secret-weapon-of-maidens-cove-for-all/ [15 February 2024].

Shisana, Olive. 'Message from the Co-chair of the South Africa Mental Health Conference', 2023. Available: https://mentalhealthconference.co.za/dr-olive-shisana/ [2 February 2024].

Tomlinson, Mark, Kleintjes, Sharon and Lake, Lori. 'Child and Adolescent Mental Health', South African Child Gauge, 2021/2022. Available: https://ci.uct.ac.za/sites/default/files/content_migration/health_uct_ac_za/533/files/Child%2520Gauge%25202021_110822.pdf [18 April 2024].

White, M.P., Alcock, I., Wheeler, B.W. and Depledge, M.H. 'Would You Be Happier Living in a Greener Urban Area? A Fixed-effects Analysis of Panel Data'. *Psychological Science*, 24(6): 920–928, 2013. Available: https://pubmed.ncbi.nlm.nih.gov/23613211/ [2 February 2024].

Wood, Michael. 'A Brief History of British Lidos – And New Hope for Their Return to Glory', *The Conversation*, 3 July 2023. Available: https://theconversation.com/a-brief-history-of-british-lidos-and-new-hope-for-their-return-to-glory-208626 [17 April 2024].

Recommended reading

Branch, George and **Branch**, Margo. *Living Shores: Interacting with Southern Africa's Marine Ecosystems*. Cape Town: Struik Nature, 2018.

Branch, George, **Griffiths**, Charles, **Branch**, Margo and **Beckley**, Lynnath. *Two Oceans: A Guide to the Marine Life of Southern Africa* (fifth edition). Cape Town: Penguin Random House SA, 2022.

Branch, Margo. *Exploring the Seashore in Southern Africa*. Cape Town: Struik Nature, 2018.

FitzGerald, Mary (ed.). *Stars of the Southern Skies: An Astronomy Field Guide*. Johannesburg: Wits University Press, 2005.

Fox, Justin *Place*. Penguin Random House, 2023.

Slingsby, Peter. *Cape Point, Simon's Town & Fish Hoek* (fifth edition). Cape Town: Slingsby Maps, 2022.

Yeld, John and **Baker**, Martine. *Mountains in the Sea: Table Mountain to Cape Point: An Interpretive Guide to the Table Mountain National Park*. Cape Town: South African National Parks, 2004.

Acknowledgements

This book comes with many thanks.

To Matthew, thank you, for everything.

To Neil Rusch, who suggested I write the book in the first place and who encouraged me when I lost steam; Franco Fong for capitulating and joining me on many a wild tidal pool swimming adventure, even in stormy weather; Nicole McCreedy, who is always the first one in; Michael Walker, who always swims with me at 6 a.m. in icy cold water and is the best person to take bad selfies with when our fingers are frozen after a swim; and Seth and Melissa for at times enduring with (mostly) good humour my desire to swim and be outdoors, and occasionally joining me in the water with marked enthusiasm. I'll make open-water swimmers of you yet!

To Julian van der Westhuizen, for the use of his camera and for always supporting me when I asked, again and again, to use it.

To Mellissa le Fevre for early-morning swims rich with laughter, and Sarah and Matthew Nissen-Dowling for their quiet support.

To Jackie Plank for her nudges, pushes, shoves and unwavering support.

To Wolfgang Grulke for his directional guidance.

I interviewed the following people, who all generously shared their extensive knowledge: Eddie D.E. Bosman, Lily Bovim, Kevin Fellingham, Barrie Gasson, Steve Herbert (Kalk Bay Historical Association), Dr Robin Lee, Andre Malan (Graaff's Pool) and Tessa Moore.

To Mark, Caitlin and the Rockhopper team for jumping in to support the vision; Tania for her fantastic design; Jay for images that raise the bar; and Lesley Hay-Whitton for her excellent editing.

Index